SHOSHANA JOHNSON

with M. L. Doyle

I'm Still Standing

From

Captive U.S. Soldier

to

Free Citizen—

My Journey Home

A TOUCHSTONE BOOK

Published by Simon & Schuster

New York   London   Toronto   Sydney

Touchstone
A Division of Simon & Schuster, Inc.
1230 Avenue of the Americas
New York, NY 10020

First Touchstone hardcover edition February 2010

TOUCHSTONE and colophon are
registered trademarks of Simon & Schuster, Inc.

For information about special discounts for bulk purchases,
please contact Simon & Schuster Special Sales
at 1-866-506-1949 or business@simonandschuster.com.

The Simon & Schuster Speakers Bureau can bring authors to your live event.
For more information or to book an event
contact the Simon & Schuster Speakers Bureau at 1-866-248-3049
or visit our website at www.simonspeakers.com.

Designed by Ruth Lee-Mui

Manufactured in the United States of America

1   3   5   7   9   10   8   6   4   2

Library of Congress Cataloging-in-Publication Data
Johnston, Shoshana, 1973–
I'm still standing : from captive U.S. soldier to free citizen—my journey home
Shoshana Johnston with M.L. Doyle.—1st Touchstone hardcover ed.
p. cm.
"A Touchstone book."
1. Johnson, Shoshana, 1973– 2. Iraq War, 2003—Prisoners and prisons, Iraqi.
3. Women prisoners of war—Iraq. 4. Prisoners of war—United States—Biography.
5. Prisoners of war—Iraq—Biography. 6. Women soldiers—United States—
Biography. 7. African American soldiers—Biography. I. Doyle, M.L. (Mary L.)
II. Title.
DS79.764.U6J64 2010
956.7044'37—dc22
[B]
2009018702
ISBN 978-1-4165-6748-6 (hardcover)—ISBN 978-1-4165-7028-8 (ebook)

Acknowledgments and Dedication

SHOSHANA JOHNSON

It took a lot of convincing before I would agree to write this book. My parents told me that people would want to hear my story. They told me that since I was the first black female ever to be held as a prisoner of war, I was obligated to tell what had happened to me. I did countless newspaper, magazine, and TV interviews when I returned home, but everyone still said I needed to write a book about the ordeal.

Now, almost ten years since the start of the Iraq War, it has become clear that they were right. It is a story that should be told.

My life has forever changed because of what happened in An Nasiriyah on March 23, 2003. One day, maybe I'll be able to get through a day when I don't think about it, when I don't wonder what I could have done to change things.

This book is dedicated to my family; my parents, Eunice and Claude Johnson; sisters Nikki and Erika, and my daughter, Janelle; nieces Devyn and Ella; all my grandparents; and to my aunts, uncles, and cousins, living and in heaven. All have been there for me through thick and thin. And in loving memory of my comrades who have given their lives in defense of our country. They are not forgotten. I have to thank my friends Dave, Ron, Joe, Jim, Edgar, and Patrick. I am here because they were there for me. Only they can truly understand.

I would also like to thank U.S. military personnel in all regions of the world for defending our freedom and for their service to this great country—especially the U.S. Marine Corps, which came to my rescue. Thanks to the city of El Paso, Texas, for its unwavering support of my family and me, to Reverend Jesse Jackson and the Rainbow/PUSH family; the Black Caucus; Fields Law Firm of Baton Rouge, Louisiana; Senator Kay Bailey Hutchinson; Congressman Silvestre Reyes; and my native country of Panama. A special thanks to all who prayed for us during our time of captivity.

Thanks to Paul Brown and Craig Wiley for their advice and care in this new world I find myself in.

A special thanks to the fantastic team at Touchstone who helped make this book happen. Especially Sulay Hernandez, who worked so hard to ensure this story made it to print. Sulay's professionalism, kindness, and sheer determination are what turned this effort from a thought to a reality.

And finally, to Joey the baby-faced Marine, who was just doing his duty. I owe my life to him and his unit. Oorah!

Acknowledgments

M . L . D O Y L E

Like most people, the first time I saw Shoshana Johnson was in a grainy video shown on CNN under captions that read BREAKING NEWS. The image of the petrified woman haunted me for days. I was working for the Army and living in Germany at the time. Thousands of soldiers in the unit I worked for were part of the same massive convoy Johnson and her fellow soldiers traveled in on their way into the heart of Iraq. News of the ambush was horrifying, and since it came so early on in the war, it seemed like a terrible foreshadowing of disaster.

According to the reports, the people who ambushed the 507th Maintenance Company, killing eleven and taking five prisoners, weren't wearing uniforms. They were mobs of civilians who overwhelmed the U.S. forces that had wandered into An Nasiriyah by mistake. Should what happened in that city have provided early clues into what would become a war of insurgency featuring roadside bombs and sniper attacks?

Early reports of the ambush seemed to blame the soldiers who had been attacked, indicating subtly that the soldiers had been lost, that they were only maintenance and support personnel and not prepared for heavy combat, and that their weapons had malfunctioned because of lack of maintenance, making it difficult for them to defend themselves. The reports seemed to supply a list of excuses why members of the best-trained military in the world could have been ambushed so successfully and why five prisoners could have been taken. The message we were to take from those reports was that the 507th Maintenance Company was ambushed because they were somehow deficient and not up to the same standards of a typical Army unit. The attack on their convoy and their subsequent defeat was an anomaly.

What we never learned were the details of the force that was brought to bear against the eighteen heavy trucks carrying thirty-three soldiers who had become separated from the main body of the convoy. The 507th wasn't attacked by a simple mob of civilians who hadn't received the message that they were supposed to welcome the U.S. forces with smiles and waves and cries of thank you. These civilians had plenty of ammunition, AK-47s, rocket-propelled grenades, and mortars, and plenty of people trained to use them. They used organized attack methods to separate the convoy and to force the heavy trucks off the roads. They had prepared for the ambush and carried it out.

Was An Nasiriyah just one of many places where the Iraqi insurgency had already taken hold?

One has to wonder what conclusions military leaders may have been able to draw had immediate blame not been leveled against the soldiers of the 507th Maintenance Company. The 507th entered the city by mistake but, in that mistake, flushed out the true nature of what the war in Iraq would become. It was never a war against Saddam and his elite Republican Guard, but a war against well-armed, well-trained, civilian-clad fanatics who knew they couldn't beat the U.S. Army in a head-to-head fight. Surprise and ambush were their best weapons. The enemy learned that lesson in An Nasiriyah on March 23, 2003, but it would be months after the ambush and the capture of Shoshana Johnson and her fellow soldiers before Donald Rumsfeld and the Bush administration would even acknowledge that we were fighting an insurgency.

As a woman who wore the uniform of the Army Reserve for seventeen years, seeing Shana in the video was like watching my worst nightmare play out. Throughout the days of her captivity, I was glued to the news, hungry for any nugget of information about the POWs. After a while, I have to admit, I was pretty convinced they were all dead. What a thrill it was to learn that they had been rescued. At the time, I never could have predicted that I would be involved with helping to tell her story.

I remember seeing her on the Jay Leno show. She was beautiful, poised, bright, and articulate. She seemed so normal, so approachable, someone everyday Americans could relate to, and I wondered, like so many others did, why Jessica Lynch had been shoved before the cameras and not this brave, intelligent woman. By the time I met Shana, she had been through a long list of positive and negative experiences, in the press, with the Army, in her day-to-day life. After all that she has been through, she still remains that normal, approachable good-hearted person I first saw on Jay Leno.

Shana has one hell of a story to tell, and I've lain awake at night hoping that I could do it justice. I prayed I wouldn't screw it up. I wanted everyone to know how much she has been through, how bravely she handled everything that was thrown at her, and what a great person she is. Shana is one powerful female.

I have to thank my agent, Liz Trupin-Pulli, and my editor,

Sulay Hernandez, for thinking of me for this project. Their belief in my ability to do this boggles the mind, and I'm grateful for their support. Thanks to Sue Silpasornprasit for her red pen. Thanks to Kathy Haley, Phil Formo, Diane Rifkin, and Larry Bangert, the original motivators. Thanks to Ruth Doyle for always having her nose in a book and teaching me the value of the word on the page. Thanks to Loran Doyle for reading the whole thing. Thanks to Dr. Loreen "Cookie" Doyle-Littles for reading and reading and reminding me that anything is possible. To my family, Larry Doyle, Becky Doyle, Reuben Sorrells, and the rest for their love and support, and most of all, thanks to Shana. You may not be comfortable with the label, but you are still a hero in my book.

Contents

1

A POW

"I'm hit! I'm hit!"

It was like a line in a movie. But I was saying it. I had felt a hard thud against my left ankle, then a searing burning sensation through both of my legs, but I had no idea how bad it was—only that I didn't have time to check it out. My legs felt torn and wrecked and I could feel a warm pool of blood forming at the bottom of both of my boots. My toes were swimming in it, and it hurt like hell. Under other circumstances, I would have curled into a fetal position, grabbed my wounds, screamed for help, been paralyzed in pain and fear, but as much as it hurt, there was too much stuff going on to pay any attention to it.

It was Sergeant James Riley's idea to take cover under the five-ton tractor trailer I had ridden across the desert. As usual, he had sounded completely confident and sure about his idea to crawl under the huge vehicle to get away from the barrage of fire that surrounded us. It might have been his stoic attitude, or maybe it was the BCGs—the Army-issue glasses that supposedly made you look so undesirable they were nicknamed Birth Control Glasses.

Those glasses and Riley's confident attitude colored everything he said with the hue of wisdom and made it easy to follow his commands, so Specialist Edgar Hernandez, the driver of the truck I rode in, and I had hit the dirt and low-crawled under there with him without thinking twice.

There hadn't been too many other options. We couldn't tell how many people were shooting at us. It could have been hundreds judging by the amount of fire. However many there were, they wanted us dead and they surrounded us. No one shooting at us was wearing a uniform. They were just men, most of them in Western clothes—shirts, jeans, athletic shoes. Some wore traditional robes and sandals. It wasn't the army I had expected to call an enemy in this fight. They were just men, angry, screaming, deadly men who outnumbered us in a big way and they were killing us, killing my friends.

We had wandered into their killing field like lost lambs. Our convoy of eighteen vehicles had driven down the narrow streets of this medium-size city. Buildings towered over us as we made several turns, stopped a few times, and were obviously confused about where we were and what we were doing. We had given them plenty of time to gather their forces and surround us. We had almost asked for this.

A constant barrage of bullets was pinging off our vehicles, nearby buildings, the ground all around us. They were lobbing mortars, and the heavy explosions made the ground leap beneath me. It had to have been like shooting down into a pen of trapped animals. We didn't have anywhere to go, no escape, and little defense. The shots were coming so close, you could hear the zipping noise they made as they whipped past us to hit something solid a fraction of a second later. I was only halfway under the truck when the bullet struck my legs. I screamed that I had been hit and Riley grabbed my arm and dragged me the rest of the way under cover. Seconds later, Hernandez took a round in the upper arm.

There was blood everywhere.

"Why isn't anyone coming to help us?" I screamed.

Riley and Hernandez ignored me, their attention focused on what was going on around us. It was a miracle we weren't all dead. Our attackers were laying down a blanket of fire from every direction and angle. My untrained assessment of the situation was that we were pretty much fucked. I had fired my weapon once from the cab of the truck—a shot I got off despite my fear, violently shaking hands, and the two-hundred-meter distance between me and the guy aiming at me with a pistol. I missed.

"Give me your weapon," Riley demanded.

I handed him my M16. He took aim and pulled the trigger. Nothing happened.

"This one's jammed, too," he said in disgust, tossing the weapon to the ground. "Piece of junk."

Hernandez fired a couple of times, but in short order his weapon became as useless as mine. Now, between Riley, Hernandez, and me, we had three M16s that wouldn't fire.

We were defenseless. Worse, I knew people were dying around us, people who were my friends. People I cared about.

I knew First Sergeant Robert Dowdy, the man we called Top because he was the highest-ranking noncommissioned officer in the unit, was dead. I had had a brief glimpse of his battered body after his vehicle slammed into the back of my five-ton. My friend Pie, Specialist Lori Piestewa, had been driving Top's vehicle and I knew she was hurt, too, hurt badly. She looked pinned inside the wreckage, blood splattered on her forehead. I couldn't tell if she was dead or alive but she wasn't moving. My friend Jessica, Private

First Class Jessica Lynch, had been riding with Pie, but I hadn't had any sight of her. I only knew that their vehicle had been hit with something like an RPG (rocket-propelled grenade), they had lost control, and they had slammed into the back of my five-ton, which left their truck a twisted pile of metal. It was apparent that anyone left alive in there was probably in very bad shape.

A bullet struck one of the huge tires of the truck that served as our shelter and air hissed out, the vehicle slowly lowering and tilting over us. Another round pierced the radiator, adding a loud hiss to the noise around us. I worried one of the rounds would find the gas tank and the whole thing would explode over us and we would go up in a ball of flame.

"Can you guys see any of our guys, anyone coming to get us?" I asked.

"Miller has a good fire position. He's taking a bunch of people out," Riley said. He still seemed calm, calculating, taking in the whole situation as if from a distance.

Everything was noise and confusion; flying dirt and black smoke obscured our vision. The stinging, metallic smell of cordite and the thick, choking smell of burning oil, plastic, and metal hung heavy in the air. I heard the people who were shooting at us calling to each other; the language was incomprehensible but the tone, the excitement in their voices that they had Americans cornered, was apparent in their speech.

It was impossible to know exactly what was going on, but there were some things I knew for sure. We were all in some deep shit, the kind of shit you only see in movies. My legs were killing me. We were about to die.

Then I saw an RPG headed for our truck. I watched as it seemed to float on air in a deadly path to the side of our vehicle. I should have screamed a warning at Riley and Hernandez, should have told them to duck, but I watched that rocket headed toward us and simply couldn't make a sound. Nothing would come out of my mouth. I cringed, ducking my head into my arms, thinking I was about to be incinerated in the approaching explosion. The round hit the side of the truck with a hollow thud and nothing happened. *A dud,* I thought, but there was too much going on to feel any relief at that stroke of luck.

"We have to surrender," Riley said. He said it as a matter of fact, as if it were a given. He scanned the area, still calm about everything, as if he thought he was starring in his own movie and wouldn't be the one to be hit in this climactic scene. I wanted to hit stop, rewind, and go back to that part that didn't have me in it, but that wasn't going to happen. I was terrified and surrendering was the last thing I wanted to do, but there was no denying that the three of us cowering under that truck had no way to defend ourselves and two of us were bleeding. Help wasn't coming. I didn't expect the cavalry to come charging over the hill. Riley's idea to surrender, an idea that was unlikely to enter any Hollywood movie star's dialogue, seemed the only option.

The shooting started to slow down, but that wasn't good news. The bullets were only coming from the enemy now. No one on our side was shooting anymore.

"They've got Miller now," Riley said. "We have to surrender. There's nothing else we can do."

The thought of surrendering petrified me. Interrogations, beatings, torture, rape—all of that flashed through my head.

My daughter.

My family.

How the hell did I end up here?

But Riley was right, we had to give up. Just as he had led us to the shelter, he slid back, then stepped out from under it, his hands raised. I held my breath, fearing he might be mowed down in front of us. After several moments no one fired and Riley remained standing, so Hernandez followed him, pushing himself out from under the truck, leaving a trail of blood behind and cradling his wounded arm. He raised his hands and waited for what came next.

I was shaking. I was saying the Lord's Prayer to myself and rustling up the gumption to push myself out from under the truck, when someone grabbed my legs and pulled me from my shelter.

And like that, I became a prisoner of war.

2

The Oath

It may seem odd now, since our country is at war on two fronts and death and injury seem much more commonplace in our world, but when I joined the Army, war was the last thing on my mind. Like so many people who enlisted pre-9/11, the Army was a place of opportunity for me, where one could gain experience, earn a living, and stack up money for college.

In the household where my sisters and I grew up, our parents monitored our grades closely because education didn't end with high school. It was expected that I would go to college, which I did as required. The problem was that I didn't have a clue what I wanted to do for a career. I switched majors several times, from physical therapy to business, and even thought about nursing for a time, but none of them stuck. With such a lack of purpose, the grades began to suffer and it didn't help that I discovered I enjoyed partying more then showing up for class. Eventually I dropped out. Despite my lack of education, I wanted my own apartment and the independence that went along with it. At times, I juggled three jobs at once trying to earn enough money to get by.

I was working in the food court of the Fort Bliss Post Exchange, serving popcorn at the popcorn stand, when I realized I had to make a change. I was scooping up the fluffy, addictive stuff popped in fat and covered in salt and butter for only a few hours a week, but that smell seemed permanent in my hair and clothes. I realized that all of the jobs I had, from serving popcorn to working in a convenience store, were jobs one might settle for if you were working your way through school, or as something extra, something to supplement your income. I was selling popcorn so that I would have money to pay rent. It simply wouldn't do.

"Shana, you need to get back to school," my aunt Maggie said one day, with that scolding note in her voice.

"I will go back," I said. "I just need some time to decide what to go to school for."

"You go to school to get an education." She repeated the familiar advice. "You're not going to get anywhere in life without it."

"I tried that," I told her. "This time, when I go back to school, I want to have a career goal. Something I can stick to."

Aunt Maggie rolled her eyes at me. "Shana, you need to stop thinking about what career you want or how much money you can make doing it. You just have to figure out what it is you love to do and do that."

I hadn't really equated a career choice with something I enjoyed doing. When I asked myself what I loved to do, the first thing, really the only thing, that stuck out without a doubt in my mind was baking. I was six years old when my aunt Joanne showed me how to make lemon meringue pie and I still have my mom's red Betty Crocker cookbook she passed down to me when I was a little girl, the one that inspired me to rummage through the cupboards, searching for ingredients to try in some new dish. One of my most memorable gifts had been an electric mixer I received on my thirteenth birthday, and in their attempt to be supportive, my sisters had swallowed down many a disaster I had concocted in the kitchen.

All of this kind of crept into my head over several days and weeks as I was still scooping popcorn at the food court. My best friend, Theresa, was working at the Baskin-Robbins stand in the same food court, and one day she showed me how to make roses and other decorations for the ice cream cakes. I enjoyed it. I was good at it. Slowly but surely I made the decision to become a baker.

When I started doing some research, the first thing I learned was that culinary arts schools are expensive, and with my grade history and the fact that I had already dropped out of college once I wasn't likely to get a scholarship or a grant handed to me. My sister Nikki had already joined the Army and was earning money for college and several of my cousins had banked plenty of scholarship money to pursue their dreams by joining one service or another. I followed their examples.

I was twenty-five years old when I raised my hand and swore to protect and defend the Constitution of the United States against all enemies foreign and domestic.

I had always considered the Army a viable option. It wasn't like there was anything to be afraid of. I had grown up with a drill sergeant in my house. I watched my dad spit-polish his boots in the evenings so he would be ready before the sun came up to go to PT (physical training) with his unit. His uniform had changed over the twenty years he served, from green khakis to the woodland camouflage BDU (battle-dress uniform) to the desert-sand BDUs, but it was always the same Army and it was a life I was fully accustomed to.

My parents, Claude and Eunice, are Panamanian. My dad

joined the U.S. Army after our family emigrated to the United States when I was five years old. My two sisters, Erika and Nikki, were born in the States and so were automatic citizens, but our family bounced back and forth between Spanish and English at home and have never lost our pride in our Panamanian culture. People take one look at our family and say we are African-American, but in truth, if our label must be hyphenated, we like to think of ourselves as Panamanian-American.

Most of the intimidating stuff associated with joining the Army was already so familiar to me it simply wasn't an issue. Our family made several PCS (permanent change of station) moves over the years because of our father's assignments. My sisters and I attended Department of Defense schools when we lived in Germany, and while we didn't like it, we knew how much red tape could be associated with a life in the Army. Some people might think it was strange to stand for the national anthem in a movie theater before the film played, but it was just a regular part of military life for my sisters and me.

I had already practiced many of the skills associated with being a soldier. While in Germany, I joined Junior ROTC, the Reserve Officers' Training Corps for high school students. We learned how to wear a uniform, practiced drill and ceremony, and even fired and maintained weapons. I knew what it was like to salute, to stand in formation, and to give the commands to maneuver troops across a parade field.

I had been raised with the understanding that a military career was one in which you could succeed based on your skills and abilities, a career where color, gender, and even nationality have little to do with your success or failure. I had watched my father move up through the ranks and my sister was an officer. Putting on a uniform was the logical thing to do.

Culinary arts school was my goal, so I enlisted with a 92G MOS (military occupational specialty). I became a cook. I thought of it as an opportunity to learn a skill I could use to improve my future, and besides, a cook was one of those "safe" military jobs—a job that didn't involve combat, one that wouldn't require me to deploy to a bunch of different hot spots around the world. I imagined that I could settle down on a military installation somewhere, cook great meals, have a nice apartment, save money, and maybe even go to school in the evenings. I would be surrounded by men, by soldiers. I hoped I might meet a nice guy, at the very least have an active social life. Not to mention that a few months of the Army's intense fitness training would help me get in shape and shed some poundage.

Like anything that one imagines, some of those things did come true, some of them didn't. I learned a skill. I had a nice place to live. I had friends and I gained confidence in my ability to take care of myself. But cooking for five hundred soldiers does not make you a chef. Rising before dawn to cook ungrateful people their breakfast does not make for much of a social life and being around food all day makes it hard to maintain a girlish figure. The most important lesson I learned, a lesson the Army was still learning when we started the war in Iraq, the lesson that took the longest to sink in, even when I had desert sand on my boots, was that there is no such thing as a "safe" Army job.

3

Into Custody

One man grabbed my ankles, one in each hand, and dragged me out from under the truck. My instinct was to struggle a bit, not wanting to suffer the indignity of being dragged from my shelter against my will, but the violent jerk on my wounded legs made me scream out in pain. Agony washed up my legs and exploded through me. Putting up a fight dimmed to nothing after that. I was helpless.

Boots, sandaled feet, weapon butts came out from everywhere, hitting my arms, my head, my wounded legs. I cowered and covered up, trying to protect my head and body, but the kicks and the triumphant shouts of the angry men around me went on and on. I have no idea how many of them there were. We had wandered into their town by mistake. We had killed some of them. They had killed some of us, and they were the victors. They were all yelling at once and I didn't understand a word of it, only that they were furious, they were wild with victory, they were really hurting me, and I wasn't convinced that they were done killing people. I thought they might literally tear me apart in their frenzy.

The pummeling continued for a long time; finally, one major kick connected squarely with my head, knocking my helmet off, and the Kevlar protection went rolling away. The man who kicked my helmet started talking excitedly, pushing and shoving others out of the way. I lay there for a second, expecting more blows to come at any time; instead he violently pulled my flak vest and the jacket of my chemical suit open, the Velcro closure ripping loudly in my ears. There was a long pause as they stared down at me, and I realized they were figuring out that I was a woman. They had seen my braids and confirmed my sex with a check that I had breasts. There was more excited talking, pushing, and shoving around me, but evidently having boobs meant the beatings would stop. There wasn't time to take much comfort in that.

A couple of the men grabbed me and hauled me to my feet, attempting to stand me up on my shattered legs.

"My legs," I screamed. "I can't walk!"

There was little sympathy from them but a lot more yelling, everyone shouting at once. I was on my feet long enough to see that Riley and Hernandez were getting the same treatment I had received. A wild-looking group of men were kicking, slapping, and pushing them around. I had glimpses of more people pouring out of buildings and gathering around us, swarming over my truck.

Our convoy had stretched out over several blocks and the truck I was in had fallen behind. I had no idea how many of our vehicles had been trapped in the fight. I could see only my five-ton and the Humvee that had struck us from behind. The Humvee that had carried Piestewa, First Sergeant Dowdy, Lynch, and two others they had picked up when their truck broke down. Five people rode in that Humvee, but none of them were moving. People surrounded it, were peering into the windshield, the doors. The truck was mangled pretty badly. I worried about my friends.

Since I couldn't see past my truck, I had no way of knowing
how many of our soldiers might have been wounded or killed.
There was still the possibility that some had gotten out, had gone
for help, would be coming back to get us. If they were coming, I
figured they'd better come pretty quick.

People were climbing into my truck, into the cab and into the
back, where all of our gear was packed for travel. A mob danced
around, waving their arms in the air, dancing to triumphant
whoops and shouts. They hauled out my rucksack and my Camel-
Bak water carrier from the cab of the truck. They would get my
CD player and my music; Missy Elliott, the Dixie Chicks, Patti
LaBelle, and Green Day. They would find my disposable camera
filled with souvenir photos of our trek across the desert. They had
the romance novels I had shoved in a side pocket and the rosary I
put in the bag at the last minute. I had packed so carefully, packed
and repacked, trying to get everything to fit. I had shopped for
body spray and hair products, worried about not being able to get
what I wanted, buying enough to last me for a while. Now it was
all gone.

I saw people emptying the truck of everything inside as flashes
between the mass of people who were pushing and shoving me
from side to side. They shouted at me, screaming and taunting.
The men who held me began to drag me across the street. They
gripped my arms roughly and hauled me away with my legs trailing behind, leaving a path of my blood in our tracks. The mass of
men parted as we went. I kept my head down, not wanting to see
the frenzied anger in so many faces; besides, I could barely see
through the pain in my legs. I was woozy with the searing agony.

They propped me up and I realized they were trying to push
me into the backseat of a vehicle. I didn't want to get in that car. I
didn't want to go with these wild-looking men.

"Riley! Hernandez," I screamed, struggling to get another glimpse of them. I was acting on instinct. I knew Riley and Hernandez were just as helpless as I was and that there was nothing they could do for me, nothing I could do for them. Maybe I yelled to let them know that men were taking me away. Maybe I yelled because everyone else around me was yelling and it wouldn't hurt to add my frightened screams to the cacophony of voices. Whatever the reason, I screamed their names like they were my saviors, my only hope. It didn't help. My captors threw me onto the backseat. It was hopeless to struggle, but I was petrified and the last thing I wanted was to be separated, to be alone and away from any other survivors from my unit.

One of the men took the driver's seat, one the front passenger seat, and another climbed into the backseat with me.

The backseat rider slapped me hard enough to snap my head back. My face stung with the indignity of it. He pushed me down onto the seat of the car, they sped away, and then their hands were all over me.

The car careened through the streets as they stripped me, first of my flak jacket and then the jacket of the chemical protection suit I had been wearing. It was a confined space. I flopped around on the backseat as we bounced over bad city roads, but somehow they were able to get my uniform and chemical suit jackets off me. I was left wearing only my brown T-shirt and bra. I felt relief that I had decided to wear a sports bra when we left on the convoy, knowing it would be harder for them to get that off me if this was something they were planning to do.

They took my dog tags. The dog tags had my name, my blood type, and my religion, Catholic, printed on the small rectangular metal disks. The disks were encased in plastic so the metal wouldn't clink together and the pair of tags was on a thin metal chain. I had been wearing those dog tags every day of my military career. They were the things that would identify my body if these wild men decided to toss me out of the car in the middle of the desert. I was afraid of being dead and unidentified, but I was more afraid of fighting them. Afraid they would tire of me, kill me, and dump my body in the road. I let them have the dog tags.

The backseat man then grabbed my breast. It was a vicious, mean grab, his entire hand taking what he could in one go. I screamed and tried to cover up, my arms wrapped around my chest. My heart and soul went into that scream. I screamed with indignation, with all the fear and anger that I could muster. His eyes got huge and he cringed away from me, as if surprised that I would actually object to the manhandling.

The scream worked. He stopped with the groping but continued to pat my body down until he found the two thirty-round magazines I had stashed in the cargo pockets of my uniform pants. He took them and seemed satisfied.

We continued to careen through the streets and I bounced around on the backseat. The men had the windows opened and they leaned out, shouting as we went, one of them brandishing an M16, maybe my M16. I didn't know what they were saying, but it was obvious they were celebrating their victory.

They had known for weeks that the American Army was set to invade their country, and in the very first days of the invasion, here we come, wandering into their town. We had obviously been lost and our frequent turns had given them plenty of opportunity to organize themselves, get the shotgun from the shed, and come running to the fight. And they had won. They had to be feeling pretty darn good about themselves. I was petrified of their fervor.

They made a turn into a walled courtyard and screeched to a stop. A gate closed behind us. It seemed quiet in the walled space.

The men got out of the car, no longer yelling and screaming. They were quiet now, their voices seeming like whispers compared to all the yelling that had been going on. The man in the backseat got out, and with someone else's help they grabbed me by my arm and T-shirt, hauled me out of the car, throwing me roughly to the ground.

Then I got my first look at an Iraqi soldier. He walked out of the building in a blue uniform, his bearing making it obvious who was in charge, and I knew this was for real now. I was in the custody of the Iraqi Army. I was alone. I started to shake.

4

Alone

I was alone the day I gave birth to my daughter.

Of course, that hadn't been part of the plan. I had been lucky in my first military assignment to Fort Carson, Colorado, since my sister Nikki would eventually join me there serving as an officer in a support unit. I expected that she would be at my side, holding my hand in the hospital as I gave birth. But Nikki happened to be in the field on unit exercises when those first pangs of labor hit.

I had gone to work as usual, long before the sun came up, to cook breakfast at the dining facility. I wasn't at work too long before I started feeling a heaviness in my stomach, pain in the small of my back, and nausea that I couldn't deny. I didn't say anything to my coworkers, only that I wasn't feeling well and that I had to leave.

I drove myself to the hospital. I have no idea how long I sat in the emergency room, only that the pain would come and go and that there seemed no end to the amount of time I sat there. When I finally got in to see the doctor, he made a cursory examination and said I wasn't ready. He sent me home.

I didn't want to go home and was afraid to drive myself, but

I hadn't any choice. I couldn't call Nikki in the field and there wouldn't have been anything she could do for me even if she had a phone with her.

I took myself home, walked around, showered, tried to take my mind off what was about to happen, and eventually I slept. At ten that night, and with strong contractions, I took myself back to the hospital. This time, it was obvious my baby was coming.

The father of my baby was deployed to Bosnia at the time of her birth. We had met in the dining facility where I worked. He was someone I talked to a lot, passed the time with. I enjoyed talking to him and we would seek each other out when we could. We made each other laugh. We were friends. We should have just stayed friends.

Our getting together was one of those things that probably never should have happened. It wasn't the right fit and I probably knew all along it wouldn't last, and it didn't. When I got pregnant, I told him, but only because he would eventually know, would see that I was going to have a child. The women in my family, my mother, my aunts, had always said you had to be ready to take care of yourself and not rely on a man to take care of you, and that was exactly what I intended to do. I didn't expect anything from him, but he would always be the father of my child. How that would play a part in my life and my daughter's life took a long time for us to figure out, but in the beginning, he didn't play a role.

I was afraid to tell my parents that I was about to have a child. I had no intention of marrying the father and every intention of staying in the Army. I was twenty-seven and had been in the Army two years and it seemed silly that I would be so worried about their reaction, but I was. I knew they would be angry and disappointed in me.

"Shana, just call your mother," my aunt Sonya said when I called her, feeling desperate and grateful to have someone to talk to about it.

"But I'm afraid," I said.

"What have you got to be afraid of? You are grown and have a job and are taking good care of yourself."

"They're going to kill me," I said.

"They are not going to kill you," she assured me. "It's not like you're fifteen."

I took her advice and called my parents the next day. They let me have it with unrestrained furor. They were both angry, my mom and dad. There were tears and harsh words. I hung up feeling terrible.

The next day, Aunt Sonya told me that my mother had called her, excited about the prospect of being a grandmother. They needed to let me know how disappointed in me they were, but after that initial anger, they have always been loving grandparents.

I guess you're never really prepared for how much labor will hurt. I cursed the man who made me pregnant; I cursed him for not being there. I cursed the fact that I was alone. I wished for my mother and my sisters.

Janelle came into the world two weeks early with only her mother to hold her. Despite my being alone, she had been born healthy and she was mine.

5

Medical Care

The Iraqi soldier had angry words for the men who had brought me to the compound. I got the impression he was angry with them for the way they had thrown me to the ground. He snapped instructions. Two young solders stepped forward and picked me up—more gently, it seemed—one man under each arm, and they practically carried me into a building and into a large room. They showed far more concern for my wounded legs than had previously been the case. They sat me gently down on the carpet.

The commander snapped more instructions at them and they left, leaving me alone with him. He closed the door, then turned and looked at me. I literally trembled in fear. I didn't know what he wanted, what he would do. No one knew where I was and I had no idea where the guys from my unit were or how many had survived.

He had a thick mustache, jet-black hair, and eyes to match. His uniform shirt was starched and tucked into his pants and a large buckle gleamed from his belt. His boots were polished to a bright shine, his pant legs perfectly creased, centered, and tucked neatly into his boots. He walked toward me, talking conversationally, as if I would understand his Arabic. I, of course, had no idea what he was saying, but that didn't seem to bother him. He kept right on talking.

He offered me a cigarette, the pack extended to me with one pulled out for me to take, his eyebrows raised. I shook my head no. He shrugged, tucking the cigarette pack back into his shirt pocket, his eyes never leaving me. He stood there looking at me for a long moment. I wondered what he was thinking. There was no way to tell. He abruptly left, closing the door behind him.

I let out the breath I didn't know I was holding and tried to stop my shaking. I sat there, straining to hear what was going on outside the door. I could hear voices, could hear people moving around, but I couldn't understand any of it. Everyone out there sounded angry, excited. Not knowing, not understanding any-thing, was driving me crazy.

The room I sat in was plain, save for the multiple carpets scat-tered around the floor. They were colorful, soft Persian-style car-pets, and I thought that my blood was ruining them. I leaned my back against the wall, my legs splayed in front of me. I looked at my wounds but had to look away. I couldn't stand to see the blood and the tears in my flesh. The awful mess that I saw there didn't seem to belong to me. The pain was more real than anything I had ever felt, but I refused to believe that the disaster I was seeing on my feet and legs was mine. The gore was too much.

There was nothing for me to do but worry, ask myself the same questions repeatedly. Where was I? What would happen to me? Where were Riley and Hernandez? Who else was alive? Who was dead?

I thought about my daughter. Before I left home, I had spent hours filling out paperwork, talking with my parents, talking to legal advisers, to make arrangements for my daughter should any-thing happen to me. At the time, I went through the steps with only a vague understanding that any of the arrangements I made would actually be needed. I had completed a will, had planned for her guardianship, planned for her finances, made her the benefi-ciary of my life insurance policies, blithely signing on the dotted lines thinking that you never knew when you might be in an ac-cident, or have some other unlikely mishap that would cause the plans to be carried out.

Well, something had happened to me. Despite my fear at my own circumstances, there was great comfort in knowing that I didn't have to worry about Janelle, that she would be surrounded by people who loved her. That she would feel at home and be safe.

It seemed like a long time that I sat there, my brain running away with thoughts of what might happen next. Waves of pain pulsed in my legs, always bringing me back to the reality of my circumstances. Then another uniformed man came in. He peered at me tentatively from the doorway as if asking my permission before stepping all the way into the room. There was a marked difference between this man and the other soldier. There was kindness in his face. I didn't fear him. He was thirtyish, medium height, and very slender. His thin mustache outlined a mouth that hid a small smile. His eyes showed concern and intelligence.

"I am the doctor," he said to me in English, spoken as if he had rehearsed the words in his head a few times before he said them. "I am to look at your legs."

I nodded okay, because he seemed to be waiting for my per-mission. He carried a traditional-looking medical bag, and with a few words over his shoulder he entered the room followed by a younger soldier who avoided looking me in the eye. The doctor gave instructions to remove my boots. The young soldier knelt down, tentatively unlaced my ruined boots, and slowly slipped them off my feet.

My desert-brown suede boots were now almost black with my blood. I could feel my blood pooled around my toes and had felt it squishing around in there with each painful step I had been forced to take. My feet were covered in blood, my socks soaked through. I was determined that I wouldn't cry or scream out in pain, and I managed to suppress the need to do those things, but it took all of my will. I moaned loudly. I was afraid to see what would be revealed under the boots. What I had seen so far was bad enough, but I forced myself to look. I needed to know how bad it was, and I was horrified.

Both legs had gaping wounds, huge ragged-looking things as big as my hand. I swooned at the sight of them. I felt like I was looking at someone else's wounds since all that blood and torn flesh couldn't possibly belong to me.

There was a large gaping hole on the outside of my left ankle, another larger hole on the inside, the ragged tears looking like raw chicken flesh. The right leg was worse. At least a one-inch hole was on the inside of my right leg above the ankle. Somehow the bullet must have taken a turn because it had come out near the back left side of my calf. It left a huge gash I could have put my fist in.

The doctor cleaned each of the four entry and exit points, dabbed away at them, and doused them in something that looked and smelled like iodine and hurt so bad it took me a long time to catch my breath after the horrible wincing pain. Even after that subsided, the pain continued to throb and tear at me. I wondered if I would ever walk again, worried that both feet would have to be amputated. It didn't seem possible that the ruin I was looking at would ever be normal again.

"You will be okay," the doctor said. "It is only soft tissue damage. Just soft tissue damage."

I knew he was full of crap. I could feel that bones were chipped or broken in my left leg, that the ragged gashes weren't just flesh, that muscle and more was involved. I didn't expect to get the truth from him. He was probably lying to me, but it seemed apparent he intended to do his best to care for my wounds. He wrapped my legs neatly in gauzy bandages and I watched as more red seeped through almost immediately. My right leg especially, with the huge gash, wasn't going to stop bleeding any time soon.

He gathered his things and gave final instructions to his assistant. Then he asked me if I needed anything.

"I need to go to the restroom," I said. I was embarrassed. I knew I couldn't get there on my own and the last thing I wanted was to be carried. My lack of mobility made me feel helpless, vulnerable, and at their mercy, but it couldn't be helped. I shuddered to think what their bathroom would be like. I had only seen men in the building, and if Iraqi men were anything like American men, there was every possibility that their toilet would be a disgusting mess. No matter what it was like, I needed to get there and I couldn't do it without help.

The doctor nodded. He directed his assistant to help as he awkwardly braced one shoulder under my arm. His nurse took the other side. They made a seat of their arms and they struggled to support me. I'm not a small woman and I knew I was a challenge for them to carry. They hauled me out the door and down a long hallway. We passed several soldiers standing around and I avoided their eyes, embarrassed by it all. I thought we would never get there. Finally, they gingerly lowered me down and I had to stand on my shattered legs. I knew I would either have to stand or I would have to ask these men to hold me up while I did my business and there was no way I was going to ask them to do that. So I stood on my wounded legs. I wanted to scream out in pain, but I swallowed it and shuffled into the washroom, closing the door behind me.

It was as bad as I expected it to be. It was a small dirty room with teal-colored tiles and a smell that wasn't pleasant. It was a squatter-style toilet; a ceramic basin, a marked place to put your feet, and a hole. There wasn't any place to wash my hands, no toilet paper, not even a seat to lower myself onto, not that I would have wanted to sit on anything in the filthy room. Since my boots and socks were ruined, I was barefoot, standing in the filth. It took me a while to maneuver myself into position, to find a way to brace myself on my wounded legs, to squat down and get the job done.

When I was finished, I fished around in my pocket for the tissue I knew I had there. Every pack of MREs (Meals Ready to Eat) comes with toilet tissue in it, and like every female soldier in the Army, I was saving the packets of tissue, knowing they would come in handy during the long convoy. I dug in my pocket and found my tissue and then my hand touched my notebook.

Holy shit! I thought. *My notebook.* The notebook pages that contained all of our mission coordinates and emergency radio frequencies and call signs and all of those things I was instructed to write down before the convoy left on the mission just in case there was an emergency. Well, I was sure as shit in an emergency now, but that information wasn't going to help me; instead it could put a lot of other people in danger.

I was holding the notebook in my hand and thinking about shoving the pages down the toilet hole when my escorts started pounding on the door. I had been in there a long time, what with all the maneuvering I had to do, and I knew there wasn't any way of stalling them further. I still considered the toilet hole, but it didn't seem that deep and there wasn't any way actually to flush anything. I couldn't trust that the pages wouldn't just float back up at some point.

I shoved the notebook back in my pocket and prayed I would have a chance later to get rid of the pages. I was terrified that someone might suddenly decide to search me. What would they think if they found all of that information? Worse, how would they use it?

The terrible thought that someone would find the notebook on me was going through my mind as they carried me back to the room. I worried that the doctor would notice how much more on edge I was. Would he suspect that something was different? My nerves were at their limit. We had been on the road in our convoy for three days with only snatches of sleep when we wandered into that city. The ambush, all those people trying to kill us, the explosions, and being shot; the whole thing had lasted well over an hour. An hour of the most intense terror I had ever experienced. Then surrendering, the car ride, the constant fear of abuse and interrogations—I had never been under such stress before. And I was bleeding, bleeding badly. I wasn't sure how much blood I had lost, but it hurt like hell. I had never seen so much torn flesh, so much blood, in my life, and this wound, this blood, was mine.

By the time the doctor and the nurse got me back to the room, I had started to tremble and shake; my teeth rattled in my head; I might even have become a little disoriented, lost a little of my sense of where I was or what was going on. I was going into shock.

The doctor slapped me. Out of nowhere and just like you see in movies when someone starts to babble and shake, he gave me a good stinging smack across the face and it worked. I stared at him, my mouth gaping for a moment, wondering why he had done it.

It took a minute for it to sink in, but the slap brought me around enough to realize that he was trying to help. I took a couple of deep breaths, trying to gain control of myself again.

"You are going into shock," he said by way of explanation. He watched me for a long moment to be sure I was actually seeing him. Then he nodded, and they left.

I was only alone for a few minutes when three more men came in, one armed with a video camera. They came in abruptly, no hesitation, and their manner, so different from the doctor's, scared me.

They assembled themselves, the man with the camera directly in front of me, the other two flanking him. The man on the right asked me a question in Arabic and the one on the left would immediately translate it to English.

I was sitting on the floor, my back against the wall, and I had just been brought out of an episode of shock with a stinging slap to the face. My legs were throbbing after trying to stand on them while I maneuvered to use the bathroom and my body was now rigid with the pain. Now these men began firing questions at me.

The man on the right said something in Arabic. The man on the left translated it into English. "What is your name?" he asked.

It may have seemed like a simple question, but even that first question was one I had to think about before I answered. Shoshana is a Hebrew name. I didn't know how these Arab men might feel about anything Hebrew, but I figured I didn't need to give them any further reason to mistreat me, so I edited my name a little and gave them the familiar version my friends and family used.

"Shana," I said. "My name is Shana."

The Army Code of Conduct is something we all learn while in basic training. There is one section in there that says, if taken prisoner, you can give your name, rank, and date of birth but that you should resist, "to the best of your ability," giving out information that could hurt your unit. Every soldier is familiar with the code and that's all well and good, but memorizing a set of rules and actually putting them into practice are two completely different things. I didn't know what I should or shouldn't say. I knew the radio call signs and emergency message key words I had written in my notebook were information I had to keep, but beyond that I would need to improvise. I just hoped the questions wouldn't get too tough. I wanted to convince them that since I was a cook and traveling with maintenance personnel, I didn't know anything of value.

But there was that guy with the video camera, and I did have that notebook in my pocket, and I didn't know what questions they were going to ask. They stood over me and asked their questions. The man on the left asked me another question in Arabic. The man on the right translated. "What is your family name?"

"Johnson," I said.

Again, the man on the left asked a question in Arabic. The man on the right said, "Where are you from?"

I told them I was from Texas, not wanting to give too many details. The whole time the questions were being fired at me, the guy in the middle was pointing the video camera directly at my face. The two men conferred with each other for a few seconds, and I watched them, first the guy on the right, then the guy on the left. Then they abruptly left.

At the time, I was surprised and relieved when they left so quickly. Evidently, this is the tape that was released to the media. This is the tape my family and all of my friends would see on CNN and every other TV channel that would confirm for them that I had been captured. I had no idea what effect my wide eyes and my need to look from one man to the other would have on everyone who saw the video. If I looked frightened, it was because I was. I was petrified, not because the men in the room were threatening me, but because I was alone and had absolutely no idea what would happen next. Not to mention that I was almost delirious with pain. If it appeared that my situation was dire on the video, that's because it was.

It hadn't been much of an interrogation and I wondered why I hadn't been asked any difficult questions. Maybe they were waiting for instructions and simply weren't prepared to handle American POWs in the very first days of the invasion. The lack of questions provided little relief. If these guys weren't ready to ask the questions, I wondered if they were waiting for help from someone else who was.

After a while, the doctor came back again, probably wondering if I needed another slap.

"You must lie down," he said. He took great pains to get me shuffled over to a sofa, to get me to lie down and elevate my feet, all to ensure I wouldn't go into shock again.

I cooperated and lay down, but moments later, I sat up again. The door opened. In walked Patrick Miller, James Riley, Edgar Hernandez, and a man I hadn't expected to see, Joseph Hudson. I was thrilled to see them, especially Hudson. His truck had been farther up in the convoy and I hadn't seen him or his vehicle in all of the melee that had ensued.

I sat there, my legs stretched out in front of me on the sofa, my bare toes pointed toward the ceiling, a worried smile on my face, but my smile faded and my heart began to ache when I kept staring at the door and no one else walked in. No one else. Was that all of us? What happened to the rest? What happened to the rest of my unit?

6

The Unit

I was stationed at Fort Carson, Colorado, the same base where my sister Nikki was serving, when it became time for me to decide whether or not I wanted to stay in the Army. I had completed my first enlistment of three years and had pretty much decided that I was done wearing a uniform. Army life hadn't been too bad, and it had been great to be near Nikki on my very first assignment, but she was a lieutenant and her military duty days were just as long as mine. I figured if I was going to stay in, I was going to need some help. I had just given birth to my daughter and raising her on my own while pulling all of my soldier duties was proving too great of a challenge. I told my career counselor that if I could take my pick of duty assignments, I might be persuaded to reenlist. He asked me where I wanted to go.

My parents and little sister Erika, along with much of my extended family, live in the El Paso, Texas, area, where a very large Army post, Fort Bliss, is located. My dad retired from the Army at Fort Bliss and my mother still worked at one of the convenience stores on the installation. Everyone, and I mean everyone, knew my mom. If you lived or worked on Fort Bliss, you knew Eunice Johnson. So I told my career counselor that if I could get Fort Bliss for my next duty assignment, I would sign on the dotted line for another three years.

I spent several years on Bliss as a kid, went to school there, had lots of good childhood memories there, but in truth, it's not a place where a lot of people want to be stationed. It's very hot and flat and not on the top of a lot of people's lists. And I had left the decision till very late. I only had thirty days left in my enlistment when my career counselor put in the request to see if I could get the assignment I had selected. In just three hours, I learned that my request had been approved.

When I was granted the transfer, I viewed it as a blessing. The prospect of being within shouting distance of so much family felt like a signal that I could finally relax a little, not worry so much about making all of life's decisions without the input of the people who meant the most to me. Not to mention that I had grown up around a huge extended family. I wanted my daughter to have that same experience. Her grandparents, aunts, uncles, and scores of cousins would be nearby to give her the same kind of family experience I had had.

My new job was to be a cook attached to the 507th Maintenance Company, a unit that maintained and repaired Patriot missile systems. The Patriot is a large surface-to-air rocket system that was credited in the First Gulf War with shooting Saddam's scud missiles out of the sky. The system looks like a big truck with a long rectangular box on the back. The box portion holds four missiles, worth about a million bucks each. To fire a rocket, the entire box is tilted up at an angle with powerful hydraulic lifts so that the box of rockets is pointed up at the oncoming target. Most of the time, that's how they sit, the truck parked in the middle of some field or desert, the rectangular box tilted up and ready to fire. It's a high-tech piece of weaponry that requires huge radar systems and all kinds of other expensive accessories to make it all work.

To keep the missiles in good repair, the 507th had people who were skilled technicians and mechanics. We also had a large section of supply and logistics folks who could find and acquire the specialized parts the Patriot required, and since the Patriot is moved around on a large truck bed, we needed a way to move them in case they broke down. Just about everyone in the 507th was licensed to drive five-ton trucks and huge wreckers that could tow these beasts and the rockets they required.

Mechanics, truck drivers, technicians, and supply specialists were the heart of the 507th. Three others and me were attached to the unit as cooks.

A normal duty day meant I would prepare breakfast, lunch, and dinner at a combined dining facility (DFAC) at Fort Bliss, where members of my unit, along with hundreds of other soldiers who lived and worked on the base, ate their meals. I spent my days at the DFAC from before the sun came up, reporting in at 5:45 A.M. and working until 5:45 P.M.; the twelve-hour days sometimes continued on weekends. I barely had time to drop Janelle off at day care before I was elbow-deep in scrambled eggs, grits, and bacon.

I had a nice routine going for a while there. I worked hard all day, but my mom worked at the Class Six store on base, where people with military identification cards could buy liquor and cigarettes and other things. Since she worked close by, she often picked Janelle up from the day-care center on base when I wasn't able to and spent time with her. Both of my parents were helpful and were there for me when I wanted their company, their advice and support. I didn't have much of a social life but I had a few close friends and I enjoyed my job as a cook.

Despite my comfortable routine, this was the spring of 2002. We were living in a post-9/11 world, and if you were in uniform, everything seemed a bit tentative, temporary, because you simply didn't know exactly where you would be in the coming months. It was difficult to make plans. My sister Nikki, after receiving only a week's notice, had been part of the first units that had deployed to Afghanistan. If it could happen to her, it could happen to me, so it was always in the back of my mind that anything could happen at any time. Your only option was to stay mentally prepared and to have a plan in place should word come that you would have to go.

The rumor mill on a military base, especially at a time of war, is always active. The units that deployed to Afghanistan were notified and shipped out very quickly. But the run-up to the war with Iraq went on for a long time. There was plenty of time for speculation and the rumor mill went into overdrive. Everyone wondered about which units would be deployed, which units would be most likely to go first, when the word would come, all of that. I worried about it but managed to convince myself somehow that it wouldn't happen to us. Almost every day someone heard something from somewhere about something that meant we were going for sure. I said out loud that I wouldn't believe it until I heard something official, but it was hard not to hear all the talk, to buy into all the rumors.

You couldn't turn on the news without hearing one debate or another about whether or not we should be going to war with Iraq, whether or not Saddam Hussein was a bad enough guy to send thousands of troops there. Dick Cheney was talking about mushroom clouds and President Bush was talking about weapons of mass destruction, and when Colin Powell talked about mobile nerve-gas units, they almost had me convinced.

At the time, I didn't know if it was the right thing to do. There was no doubt in my mind that Saddam was a bad guy. He had tortured and killed thousands of people. He had invaded Kuwait, which resulted in my dad and thousands of U.S. troops getting deployed to straighten the situation out. Saddam was a bad guy. There was no question about that.

But as hard as they tried, the Bush administration hadn't convinced me that Saddam had anything to do with 9/11 or that he had any connection to Osama bin Laden. We already had thousands of troops in Afghanistan and that war wasn't over yet, not by a long shot. We hadn't caught bin Laden and those were the bad guys who had actually attacked us. I thought sending troops into Iraq was going to divert our attention from that effort. I simply didn't see the point.

Considering all the time the administration was spending trying to convince us it was the right thing to do, it seemed pretty clear that we would be going to war with Iraq. In the end, I honestly didn't have a lot of time to think about the right or wrong of it. I only knew that if my unit was called up, I would have to be ready to go no matter if I agreed with the war or not.

As a cook, I wasn't around most of the unit on a day-to-day basis. I spent my duty hours in the kitchen, preparing and serving meals to people who weren't part of my unit, working most closely with the three other cooks from the 507th. As far as the rest of the unit was concerned, I knew their faces, they said hello in the chow line, and we got together for PT and formations and then went about our daily work. There were times when we were together for mandatory training, when we were brought together for unit functions, picnics and games, holiday parties, and the like, but on most days, each section of the unit went about their business, not mixing too much. At the end of each day, we all went home to our families, to the regular lives we tried to lead outside of uniform.

When word came that we would deploy, all that changed. We didn't have an exact date for departure, but we did have a long list of things we had to accomplish before we left. The entire unit scrambled to get all of our required training and preparation done as quickly as possible. We were in classes together for days on end, spent time waiting together, moved from one event to the next together, and pulled various kinds of unpleasant duties together. That old adage "Hurry up and wait" is still alive and well in the Army. You tend to fill the time you spend waiting with talking. It only made sense that we would get to know each other better, would begin to gel as a team.

The entire unit became closer, it was true, but of the eighty-two soldiers that deployed with the 507th, nine of us were women. All of us women knew we would be living together when the time came, would probably share a tent in Kuwait and wherever in Iraq we finally ended up, so we naturally came together in our male-dominated world. We shared stories, shared our gripes and worries, talked about the men in our lives and the children we would leave behind.

Lori Piestewa and Jessica Lynch and I were in each other's company much of the time. Lori told us to call her Pie. She was a smart and strong Hopi Indian woman who had no idea how pretty she was. She was always calm when things got stressful and confident that she could get through whatever life tossed at her. A natural soldier, a warrior really, she always did well in the training classes we were required to take. She was the kind of person you wanted at your back when things got tough.

Lori's roommate, Jessica, was a girlie girl, always taking the time to make sure her hair was just right and her makeup was applied perfectly. You would look at Jessica and wonder why she joined the Army. Why would such a petite little thing want to wear a uniform and drive big trucks? She said she wanted to bust out of her small town and earn money for college so that she could become a teacher. Whatever her reasons, and however small she might be, she'd pick up that rifle, drive that truck, run the miles, do the push-ups, do whatever the Army asked of her.

And we were asked to do a lot in those days as we prepared to leave. We met with legal teams to review our wills and other legal matters, like Janelle's guardianship paperwork, to ensure all were in order. We had medical and dental checkups, took refresher classes in first aid, and received a series of shots if we needed them. Classes about searching vehicles, pulling guard duty, how to operate the complicated new radios many of the vehicles had, map reading, weapons qualification and classes about chemical attacks, what to do, how to don the chemical suits . . . the list of things we needed to relearn went on and on. And even through it all, I kept thinking none of this would really apply to me. I was a cook. I would be in the rear, in a secure area. I wouldn't need to know all of this stuff.

Aside from all the classes, we had to inventory our equipment and prepare our trucks for shipment. There were long days of paperwork, shipping, packing, and briefings. We filled the between times with speculation about what life would be like, living in a tent, not having the conveniences of home, going to war. It is a hard thing to wrap your head around, the notion that you are going to war. Since the First Gulf War, soldiers have been going to Kuwait on training missions and the like, so we had some information about what the staging base would be like, but no one had been into the heart of Iraq and we all wondered about it, wondered if we would have to go.

My family seemed very calm about the whole thing. My father had deployed to the First Gulf War. He had been to Kuwait, where I was headed, he knew what I could expect there, and maybe there was some comfort in that. But he was frustrated by the whole thing.

"My daughters wouldn't be fighting this war if they had let us finish what we started the first time," he would say.

I listened to the talk of war but it didn't seem to connect in my head. I was a cook. War wasn't part of my job. I was preoccupied with making mental lists of all the things I needed to do to ensure I was ready to leave and that my daughter was ready.

Pie worked in the personnel office of the unit and she helped me with my family care plan. As a single parent, I was required to maintain a plan for my daughter should anything happen to me. The one thing I didn't have was assurance from Janelle's father that he wouldn't kick up a fuss about custody of her in the event of my death. We weren't a part of each other's life and I didn't want to worry about my daughter ever getting snatched away from the family she already knew and loved. He was stationed in Korea at the time, but it didn't take much to convince him. I was able to get his signature on the necessary paperwork and having that detail taken care of was a relief to the whole family.

Pie was a big help in getting all of that done. She knew what she was doing and I had confidence that all of my paperwork would be in order with her watching over it.

Jessica worked in supply. The days at Fort Bliss before we left on the deployment were crazy for her as she ordered and issued stuff left and right. Jessica and Pie and I would talk about the war, about how cooks and personnel clerks and supply folks would just get left in Kuwait probably and that we weren't really going to war, we were just going in support of the war. That made sense to us, so we stuck to that logic.

Jessica and Pie were very close, called each other "roomie," and spent most of their time together. You'd rarely see one of them without seeing the other close behind. Sometimes I think it was a good thing that they were together during the ambush, that there is some comfort in knowing they had each other during the attack. Of course, I had no idea what had happened to them. I saw the mangled mess of their truck, saw Lori's bloodied face, but I still hoped they were both okay. When they didn't arrive at the prison with the rest of the guys, I feared for them both.

7

The Men

Miller, Hernandez, Riley, and Hudson were led into the room and told to sit down on the carpets. They looked dog tired. It was maybe 10 A.M. at this point. We had wandered into the village around 6:30 in the morning after we had been driving for three days straight with just a few hours of snatched sleep when we could get it. I was exhausted, and they looked as exhausted as I felt. It was still morning, and so far, it had been an extremely stressful and long day.

The men were covered in sand and you could tell that some of them had gotten the same kind of beating I had. Hernandez had blood on his face. He had been shot in the arm and his wound was untreated and still bleeding. Hudson had been shot twice but I didn't know it on first glance. He was bloody but walked into the room without help. He looked pissed off. They all looked pissed off. They glanced at me as they entered the room and I could see they were surprised and relieved to see me there. They had been just as much in the dark about my whereabouts as I was about theirs.

I wanted to ask them what they had seen, where they had been, but there were armed guards around us, mean-looking guys in civilian clothes with AK-47s. I figured I could wait to talk to them. Just knowing they were alive thrilled me. I fought back tears. I wasn't alone anymore.

I couldn't shake the feeling, though, that we were it. We were the only ones who had survived. The faces and names of everyone else in the unit flew through my head. It was too much to contemplate that they were all dead.

The guys were seated and the guards offered them cigarettes. It became a familiar routine for the cigarettes to be offered immediately. Riley took a cigarette but the rest of us turned them down. They went through the whole routine of lighting the cigarette for him, then the guards stood around us smoking and watching. After a long pause, they started asking the question that would become familiar as well, the one they would all ask. "Why you come to Iraq?"

"Because we were ordered to," was the response we each gave. We used different words and tried different tactics, but we all basically said the same thing. Our captors weren't satisfied with that answer.

"You hate Saddam?" one of them asked. "You hate Iraqis? You want to kill Iraqis?"

"I'm a cook," I said, over and over again. "I had to come. I had to do what I was ordered to do."

"I came to fix stuff," Miller said. "I won't hurt them if they don't hurt me."

He seemed calm about it all, reluctant to talk but answering the questions the best way he could.

They must have seen defiance in Sergeant Riley's eyes, or maybe it was because he was the highest ranking of us, or he simply wasn't as convincing in his answers, but they all seemed to target him. They asked him, over and over, the same question, "Why you come to Iraq?" They looked threatening. They tried to intimidate him with their weapons, with shouting at him. The shouting made me cringe and I worried that Riley might be going too far. He stuck to his guns, never backing down, looked them in the eye, and answered the only way he was going to answer. He told them he was a soldier and he was doing what a soldier was ordered to do. I was a little awed by his ability to stand up to the onslaught and scared to death that at some point they would stop challenging him and make an example of him.

The guards finally tired of the game and left us alone but stayed in the room with us. The doctor came back and looked at Hernandez's and Hudson's wounds. He cleaned them up and bandaged them with the same care he had used with me. When he was finished with the dressings, he offered us pain medication. We all refused it and the doctor wanted to know why.

"I refuse to take anything if I don't know what it is," said Hudson. "Show me the pamphlet that goes with that drug," he demanded.

I was shocked that he would make such a demand but even more surprised when the doctor, without flinching, produced the paper. Hudson read it over but still refused to take the medication. Hernandez took the drug, but I followed Hudson's lead and refused to take it.

"No, you have to take it," the doctor said to me. "You are showing symptoms of shock. You must take the medication."

I didn't want to take it but I could understand the wisdom of his advice. If you asked me today what it was they gave me, I couldn't tell you, but it definitely worked. He gave me an injection in the hip and in minutes I was feeling no pain. I seemed to float

in and out of it, seeing what was going on around me but not really feeling like I was there.

"We take you to hospital now," the doctor said.

A litter was brought in and I gingerly lay down on the simple
strip of canvas stretched between two wooden poles. The men
were stood on their feet, their hands tied behind their backs. The
guards stood vigilant watch over them as they shuffled out the
door. Two men picked up my litter and were about to follow the
men out of the room when the doctor leaned down and whispered
to me.

"Your blond friend is alive. She is at the hospital."

Lynch! Jessica Lynch was alive. I'm not sure what surprised
me more, that Lynch was alive, or that the doctor had told me the
news.

8

Camp Virginia

I was so bored in Kuwait. There was absolutely nothing for me to do. Our meals were either MREs or provided by a dining facility manned by civilian workers, which meant that I didn't have a job to keep me occupied. Now and then I would be sent to pick up the MREs that were issued to us, but most of the time I had to look for work just to keep myself busy.

Lynch worked supply and Pie worked in administration and had lots of tasks to accomplish, so sometimes I would hang out with them, just for something to do. Sometimes I'd pick up a few of their errands, help them out where I could. Lynch picked up and dropped off laundry, arranged for supplies, did paperwork. Pie had to sit in the Command Post (CP) most of the day, answering phones and manning the radios, delivering messages, filling out paperwork. Now and then, I would sit in for her so that she could run errands and get out of the CP from time to time.

All nine females in the unit lived in the same tent. We would sometimes eat meals together, walk to the showers together, and talk about our lives, our loves. We talked about Pie's two kids and my daughter.

Before we left Fort Bliss, I had tried to set Lynch up with a guy I thought would be perfect for her.

"I already have a boyfriend," she told me. When I asked her who he was, she blushed and refused to tell. Even while we were in Kuwait, she kept that secret to herself.

"Let me borrow some of that good-smelling stuff you have," she asked me one day, all excited.

"My body spray? Why, do you have a date?" I teased.

I was surprised when she said yes, but she still wouldn't reveal who the lucky man was. I gave her a quick spritz-down of the body spray I had loaded up on before we left the world back home and she went off to her date in her combat boots and desert BDUs feeling a little more like a woman. I found out later who the boyfriend was, of course. I'm not sure why she was so secretive about it, maybe just wanting to avoid the gossip since Sergeant Ruben Contreras was in another unit that was also in Kuwait.

But going on dates certainly wasn't an everyday thing. Most of the time we sat around, did a bunch of administrative stuff, performed maintenance on our vehicles and equipment, spent lifetimes standing in line for the telephone, and made frequent trips to the tiny little post exchange (PX), where we spent hours poring over the meager goods on the shelves just for something to do.

Some of our time was spent in classrooms where we were given courses about Iraq, about some of the inherent dangers of the place, like the indigenous insects, the poisonous snakes, basics of the local flora and fauna. We learned about the dangers of the heat of the day and the potential for frigid temperatures at night. We learned some of the high and low points of Iraqi history, a little about the people and culture. They were trying to give us some background about the place and the people we would be up against.

Some of the classes were refresher courses about soldier skills like radio protocols, map reading, what to do in the event of a chemical attack. Back at Fort Bliss, we spent a lot of time on a rifle range. In basic training, I had just missed earning an expert marksmanship badge and I wanted to make up for that near miss.

There are three skill levels when it comes to weapons qualification. You could qualify as marksman by hitting twenty-six targets out of forty. You could score sharpshooter by hitting at least thirty-three out of forty. Or you could be considered an expert by hitting at least thirty-eight targets. If you hit forty targets you would have a perfect score. I was determined to have fired expert by the time I left for Kuwait.

I spent hours on the range, practice firing and volunteering to take more and more opportunities to fire at targets. The Texas heat was intense out there. There wasn't any shade and the sun seemed to reflect off the sand and rocks around us. By the time I left the range, I had burned my nose from the sun and from the heat of the weapon I was holding against my face. I did end up firing expert, but since we weren't firing for record, the score would not be noted in my personnel file and I would not be able to wear the expert badge. I knew it wasn't a recordable weapons qualification, but we were headed into a war zone and I wanted to make sure I knew what I was doing with the weapon I would be carrying. I felt like I had accomplished what I had set out to do when I finally left the range.

There must not have been a weapons range available for us to use in Kuwait because we did all of our range training in Texas. Not having a range didn't stop someone from deciding that we needed to have a refresher class on the use of a .50-caliber machine gun. We couldn't actually fire the thing, but an instructor came to one of our tents and set up the weapon, and we were given a classroom version of how to operate it. I'm not sure how useful the class was since we couldn't actually point it at anything and pull the trigger. I guess it was better than nothing.

Aside from our weapons training, we didn't get any training either in Kuwait or back in the States that would really prepare us for combat. We didn't get any training on urban battle, nothing about battle tactics, what to do in case of ambush, how to really fight when and if the time came. We had all learned basic soldiering skills in basic training and in other courses in our military careers, but we weren't infantry soldiers. We weren't combat troops. We were combat service support troops and we left Camp Virginia thinking that was the role we would play, in support of the combat soldiers, not in the middle of it ourselves.

Now that we were actually deployed and in Kuwait, the rumor mill continued to work overtime. Everyone speculated about what would happen next.

Some rumors had us moving into central Iraq, others that some of us would go, but support staff, people like me, would stay in Kuwait away from the fighting. I was hungry for any morsel of information that would reinforce that nugget of a rumor. Camp Virginia was sprawling and ugly, hot and primitive, but it wasn't a battlefield; it had a small PX, decent showers, and a place I had already turned into my personal hooch. Staying put was what I wanted to do and any rumors I heard that reinforced that desire were the rumors I chose to believe.

There were a lot of reasons to believe them. I was a cook but there wasn't any place for me to cook anything in Kuwait and the same would be true in the middle of Iraq. We would eat MREs or get our meals from kitchens contracted by the Army because that was how the Army worked nowadays. And the mechanics who actually worked on the Patriot missiles had already been assigned and transferred to the units with the Patriots. Those of us left over didn't have a single thing to do with the actual missiles. We were simply there in support and there was no reason we couldn't provide that support from right there in Kuwait. Why should we go anywhere? Leaving Kuwait would have just been stupid. I chose to believe someone would come to their senses at some point and leave us where we were.

Another thing that kept us all busy was trying to keep our equipment working. Our SINGARS (single-channel ground-air radio system) radios, the ones we could use to communicate with higher headquarters, would break down all the time and it was impossible to get parts or even find the folks with the expertise to repair them. Many of our trucks were running only because someone had devised some way to jury-rig them into operation. We would order parts and request new equipment but none of this would come to us. The units that were considered "combat" troops got all the new stuff. We didn't see any of the shiny new stuff the war fighters were getting. We were like the redheaded stepchild. Our equipment was secondhand and falling apart and we were supposed to be satisfied with that.

The days crawled by and we still didn't know what we would be doing, where we would be going. Lynch refused to eat, not liking the MREs, not wanting to eat in the dining facility. She would buy junk food at the PX, Snickers bars and chips and other candy, and tried to survive on that.

"You gotta eat," I would say to her. "You can't keep losing weight like this."

"You'll never get her to eat," Pie said in her clipped and to-the-point way. "She'll refuse. Won't do you any good. Might as well leave her be."

Pie was right. Lynch wouldn't eat. I was sure she weighed

less than a hundred pounds by the time we did finally learn that we would be leaving by convoy along with the rest of the combat troops and moving into the heart of Iraq. When I heard we would be leaving, I kept thinking how stupid, how unnecessary it was. We didn't have a role to play. At the time I didn't understand why we were being ordered to go and I still don't understand it.

The last time I saw Lori Piestewa, she looked as if she were unconscious, bloody, trapped in the twisted metal of her truck. I knew that Jessica Lynch was also trapped somewhere in that wreckage. They were my friends. I had been afraid for them, worried they were both dead, but now I knew that at least one of them was alive.

9

Movement

As soon as I had the opportunity, I told the men about Lynch. It was as they were loading us into the van that served as our ambulance that I was able to whisper to them, "Lynch is alive."

I'm sure the doctor had no idea what effect that news would have on me, or he wouldn't have told me. I was ecstatic. I figured if Lynch was alive, there was a chance Pie was, too. I wanted so badly for them both to be okay. Of the three of us, I was the highest-ranking female and I couldn't shake a feeling of responsibility for them. Sure, I knew that in the ambush, there was little I could have done for them, but that didn't mean that I still didn't feel responsible somehow for what had happened to them.

All of this flew through my head as we were loaded into the ambulance. I had been carried outside on a litter but the van wasn't equipped like a real ambulance, so I was made to stand up and climb into the van myself. I was barefoot. My feet were too swollen, and anyway, my boots were ruined by all the blood that had covered them. Any discomfort I felt in my feet from the rocky ground was nothing next to the pain in my legs as I climbed into the van and shuffled onto a seat in the back. The men climbed in and we sat facing each other on benches, the men leaning forward to accommodate their hands tied behind their backs. The canvas litter was folded up and lying on the floor between our feet. Even Hernandez, who had been shot in the arm, had his hands tied behind his back.

Two men climbed into the front of the ambulance and two rode in the back with us. They were all armed with automatic weapons and pistols strapped to their thighs. They wore civilian clothes and they looked watchful and serious as we drove at what seemed like breakneck speed through the streets of the city. I wondered if they were regular Iraqi soldiers wearing civilian clothes or if they were civilians like the people who had ambushed us. They seemed like professionals and I wondered why they weren't in uniform.

The pain medication, whatever it was, began to work in earnest as we drove. I floated in and out of consciousness. I could see and hear everything that was going on around me, but it didn't seem to register in my brain. I snapped to reality, though, when we heard the sound of multiple explosions. I looked at the men, and they were all wide-eyed, trying not to smile.

"Armor," Hudson whispered.

Oh, thank God! I thought to myself. *They are coming to get us. We'll get rescued soon. We're going to get out of here.* Hudson was hearing tanks and tanks always had infantry with them. The ground pounders would come get us, I was sure of it.

The sounds of the attack made me feel almost giddy with hope, but it made our Iraqi captors inside the van very tense. We could hear automatic weapons fire, multiple loud explosions; we could feel the ground shake with the impacts even through the floor of the van. It had to be the Marines, I thought. At around dawn, we had passed a long column of tanks belonging to Marines just before we turned into the city. There had been a lot of tanks and lots of Humvees with crew-served weapons, and they were Marines. I figured that had to be who was attacking the city.

The guards decided we couldn't stay on the road. They made a quick turn into a gated courtyard and stopped. The back doors of the van were thrown open. Two of the guards grabbed the litter while the men were hustled out of the van. I moved as quickly as I could at the guard's urging and, once outside the van, lay back down on the litter and we rushed into a building. The guards were on edge and they moved quickly along the hallway, bouncing me up and down on the litter, shouting instructions as they pushed and moved us along down a hallway.

They crowded us into a small room, just setting my litter down on the floor. They made the guys sit down then they quickly closed the door, locking it behind them.

We were alone together for the first time, but that seemed minor compared to the attack on the city that had begun in earnest. The crump of massive explosions rocked the building. Long bursts of automatic weapons fire were drowned out by the scream of other incoming rounds. War was happening out there and Americans were bringing it. The same thought kept going through my head. *We're going to get rescued right now. I'm going to get to go home right now!*

But the rescue never came. After a while, we started talking about what we had seen during the attack, what we knew, what we still didn't know.

Riley and Miller had been riding together and had been moving up and down the convoy line during the attack. They had seen more than the rest of us. They started naming names. The ones they knew were dead. Every name was a greater shock to me. So many good people, so many of the ones who had kids and people waiting for them, had died. They had picked up Private Brandon Sloan somewhere along the convoy route. Sloan, only nineteen years old, had been shot in the head and died quickly, they said, in the heat of the ambush.

Sloan had a very slow southern drawl that people liked to imitate and make fun of. I had always admired his ability to shake off the teasing, not get angry or resentful that folks chose to pick on him. He remained a good-hearted young man, and at nineteen years old he was far too young to die.

Chief Warrant Officer Johnny Villareal Mata, the man we called Chief Mata, was the man who somehow, when everyone else was looking filthy and tired, produced a stiffly starched uniform in the middle of the desert and wore it proudly. Chief Mata was always looking crisp and spotless. Mata had been riding with Hudson. Hudson said Mata had been firing like crazy; even after being shot, he continued to take the fight to the attackers.

"He saved my life," Hudson said.

But Chief Mata had died in the truck next to Hudson. Hudson had been shot twice and was forced to surrender.

I had walked next to Specialist James Kiehl when we left our families at the deployment center. Kiehl's wife, who was seven months pregnant at the time, had been red-faced and bawling. She stood there waving at him, racked with great heaving sobs as our bus left, her belly looking huge on her small frame.

"I wish she wouldn't cry," Kiehl had said.

I wished it for him, too. Her grief at his leaving was hard to watch and I knew the news of his death would be devastating for her. Kiehl had been baptized while we were at Camp Virginia, just two weeks before we had left on the convoy, as if he knew he wouldn't be coming home. He didn't live to see his first child.

Kiehl's good friend Specialist Jamaal Addison had done what so many soldiers have done over the years—married his sweetheart before he left for war. He also had a young son who would never see his father again. Addison was a quiet man who would say, "Let's just do this thing so we can go back home."

Riley had seen Private Ruben Estrella-Soto die. Hernandez and Estrella were best buddies and Edgar refused to believe he was dead. The two men hung out together and spoke Spanish to each other.

"What did you see? How do you know he's dead?" Hernandez demanded. Riley didn't like being the one to deliver the bad news, but I could tell from his face that Estrella and the guy who was also riding in his truck, Private First Class Howard Johnson III, were probably both dead.

"He's gone," Riley said.

"No, you saw it wrong," Hernandez said.

"I saw their truck get hit with a rocket and flip over," Riley went on. "There's no way they could have survived."

They had been driving a five-ton tractor trailer loaded with heavy equipment. If that thing had flipped there was little likelihood they could have walked away from it. Edgar sat there shaking his head, refusing to believe his best friend was dead. He and I had just spoken with Estrella and Johnson while in the town, right before the attack happened. It was too hard to believe that they could be alive one minute and dead the next.

There were others we didn't know about for sure and I could only assume they were dead. It was all too much. I cried for them. I looked at the men still with me, thinking we could be the only survivors. How did we deserve to be alive when so many of the good ones had died?

Hudson wasn't going to sit around and cry. He got up, started checking out the room, maybe looking for a way out. Looking for a way to get us all in trouble is what I thought, but I couldn't fault him for his nervous energy.

Riley scooted over to me and looked at my wounds. Even though I wasn't in much pain, the bandages were already soaked through.

"These don't look so good, Johnson," Riley said.

"Yeah. I pretty much knew that," I said.

"You've got to stop all this bleeding."

"Do you think we'll get rescued now?" I asked him. The sounds of battle going on outside were the sounds of hope to me. I kept thinking a Marine would put a boot through our door any second and tell us we were safe, we were going home. I was so sure our ordeal would be over just like that. Riley wasn't convinced. He didn't say anything as he went back to sit in his place by the wall.

They left us there for hours. The battle outside subsided, then kicked up again, but never really got close to where we were. Suddenly the door was flung open and the men who had brought us came in with small bowls of rice. They thrust the food at us, saying, "Eat, eat." I wondered if they had had to learn the word in order to issue the instruction. It was the first food they had given us and I was grateful for it. We ate silently with our fingers.

At some point I had to go to the bathroom. It was so frustrating and embarrassing to ask, but it couldn't be helped. Someone knocked on the door to ask the guards for permission for us to go, and then Miller and Riley, making a seat with their arms, carried me to the bathroom. They strained under my weight. The hallway was long and I felt sorry for the bother, sorry for having to ask them to help me like that. The bathroom, if you could call it that, wasn't any better than the last one I had used. My tissue supply was quickly dwindling and I still had that damn notebook to worry about.

By the time we got back, the battle sounds were growing more distant and my feelings of hope were slowly being replaced by feelings of fear. The rescue I had wished for hadn't happened. I was still a POW and there was every possibility that we wouldn't be going home for a long time. So far, there hadn't been any long interrogations and our guards had been reasonable, not too aggressive or threatening. But I still had a notebook full of coordinates and radio call signs in my pocket, and while I knew I didn't know anything strategic in nature, that didn't mean I wouldn't be asked those things with the expectation that I was holding something of value back.

With thoughts like this going through my head, the guards came back. They told us to get up and they tied the men's arms behind their backs again. They took us outside, where a large black SUV was waiting. We couldn't all fit in the back, so they crowded the men into the back of the SUV, facing each other, their backs hunched and their knees bunched together. They lay me on the backseat of the truck and one of the guards got into the seat with me.

As soon as the door closed we took off through the streets again. I didn't know where we were going, but it seemed logical that they would be taking us to Baghdad. So far, these guys had taken us from place to place, handed us off from one group to another, and no one had seemed in charge. It made sense that they would take us to a headquarters somewhere, somewhere where a real interrogation would take place—someplace that was equipped to handle prisoners.

The thought of going to Baghdad petrified me. Saddam and his two sons, the men so well known for their torture and brutality, were in Baghdad. The war was in Baghdad. It was the last place in the world I wanted to go.

felt for my dad. I'm not sure how our mother got through those days. I wonder how she functioned with her husband so much in harm's way and with teenage daughters driving her crazy with questions and their own worries.

From the time the ground conflict started to the time the war was declared over was only a few days, but they were days our family spent glued to the television, hungry for word of what was going on. We were relieved by how quickly it was over and we anxiously waited to hear when he would be home. I was a senior in high school at the time, and my dad had assured me he wouldn't miss my upcoming event.

"I don't know when we're leaving, but I'll be home for your graduation," he told me.

"Do you know that for sure?" I asked, not thinking he had the power to make such a promise.

"Our battalion commander has a daughter in the same class as you," he assured me. "He says he'll be home for her graduation. If he'll be home by then, I'll be home by then."

Sure enough, he was able to come home in time for my commencement ceremony.

I couldn't help but think about my dad during those first days at Camp Virginia in Kuwait. I knew that he had been in Kuwait, not on the same base I was on, but he had walked the same desert, felt the same searing heat, seen the same yellow-gold sunset over the flat brown plains, and he had made preparations to go face-to-face with the same people we were preparing to confront.

It had taken us forever to get there. By the time we finally boarded the plane for the flight, we were as ready as we were ever going to be. We had spent so much time planning and packing, saying good-bye to family and friends, that by the time we actually stepped aboard the plane, filing in formation with our single

10

Making the Trip

My dad had spent twenty years in uniform, and service in the military was good, honorable work in his mind, but he had already watched one daughter leave to fight the War on Terror. Now here we were, at another deployment ceremony. Flags were waved, speeches were made, photos taken, and tears shed. It was my turn to leave and my father didn't like it, especially since I was going to a fight he felt we should have finished the first time. It was February 17, 2003.

He had deployed to the First Gulf War, a member of the Third Armored Cavalry Regiment. It was a unit we knew would be in the center of the fight, and to make matters worse, my father served as a chemical specialist when he deployed. I had been a teenager then, in high school, and our entire family had spent weeks worrying about him. We heard the reports of the scud missiles coming in, the reports that Saddam had chemical weapons, that he had used them on his own people, and the world wondered if he would have the audacity to use the same weapons against his enemies. *Worry* does not describe the anxiety we all carry-on bag, we were just looking forward to the next phase.

My unit boarded that plane a much tighter group of people than we had been before. We had spent weeks in training together, hours and hours of work in preparation to go, and now we would be living together. I knew all of them much better and they knew me. We joked around, played spades, read books and magazines, watched portable DVD players, and listened to music, escaping behind a set of headphones into our own personal reveries.

The flight was long, longer than any other flight I'd ever taken. To keep us from getting too bored, they filled our time with food, meals and snacks, and more meals. The hours dragged on. I slept some, but mostly I spent the long hours wondering what life would be like when we got to where we were going.

We finally arrived late at night, the airfield pitch-black and colder than I expected it to be; a crisp night air whipped around us as we exited the plane down the long exterior stairway. We were met on the tarmac by a welcoming party that consisted of a military police Humvee with a .50-caliber machine gun mounted in the turret and a long line of civilian buses and a couple of trucks for our baggage and equipment. The sight of the fully loaded gun, with the ammunition belt so obviously leading from the weapon, made my stomach clench. We had arrived in a war zone.

I somehow got selected to help unload baggage. I couldn't believe that after the long ordeal that was our flight, we would have to do the work of unloading the plane ourselves, but we were put to the task and we did it the way the Army does most things, as a team. We were directed into the belly of the plane, where we started shifting all of our luggage onto big trucks. It was strange being in the luggage compartment of the huge jetliner, but the novelty quickly wore off as we built up a sweat tossing overstuffed duffel bags around.

My bags, the ones I had packed and repacked a dozen times, were somewhere in the pile of hundreds that looked exactly alike. Some people had tied scarves around the tops or striped the bags with brightly colored duct tape, attempting to give their green duffel something unique to set it apart from the crowd.

My two duffel bags, with my name and Social Security number stenciled boldly on the side, were full of my uniforms and carefully wrapped new bottles and jars of hair-care products and Victoria's Secret body spray. I had several matching girlie-looking bra-and-underwear sets and lots of lotions and bath gels. When you wear a uniform and combat boots, it's nice to have things that make you feel like a woman, things to remind you of your feminine side. I had stocked up on all the goodies knowing it would be some time before any of my supplies could be replenished.

My trip to Victoria's Secret was one of the last things on my list of errands to run as I was preparing to deploy. My sister Erika came with me. We headed straight to the mall when I got off work, so I was still in uniform as I bought the sprays and lotions in quantities of two or three and even more when it came to new underclothes. The saleslady, a short Hispanic woman, made a comment about how much I was buying. When she learned that I was deploying to Iraq, she was horrified.

"You should not go there," she said, her eyes wide and her hand covering her mouth in shock. "I have a very bad feeling about it."

"It's okay," I told her. "I'll be gone for six months or so and I'll be back." I smiled at her to let her know I wasn't worried, but she didn't seem the least bit reassured. In fact there were tears in her eyes.

"But it's dangerous," she said. "I have a very bad feeling about this."

I was surprised by how upset she looked. She was a complete stranger and she seemed truly distraught that I would be heading to the war zone.

My uncle Al had dire warnings for me as well.

"I don't like this at all," he said to me in one phone call. "You need to be careful over there. Don't let your guard down."

My uncle had been in the Vietnam War and had suffered from nightmares long after he came home. At the time of our phone call, I was sure I would have an uneventful six-month deployment. When I look back on those conversations now, it surprises me how close the Victoria's Secret saleslady and my own uncle came to predicting what would happen to me.

I was allowed to bring one set of civilian clothes and I had chosen carefully: my favorite pair of Doc Martens, my best-fitting pair of jeans, and a pullover knit shirt with a collar. I also packed plenty of what just about every soldier packs, especially on a deployment where few amenities are expected . . . lots of presweetened Kool-Aid and bags of beef jerky.

I had my eye out for my own bags as we labored in a daisy chain, tossing the bags down the line, and made rapid work of emptying the plane. It wasn't too long before we were boarded onto buses for the ninety-minute ride to Camp Virginia. The buses had curtains over the windows and I wondered if they were meant to hide us or to hide the country from us.

I pushed the curtains aside and watched the desert fly by. It looked a little like Texas scrubland, flat, open brownness with small shrubs and bits of grass cropping up here and there. The road was long and straight with few cars or vehicles of any kind. We passed single-story buildings, whitewashed and dilapidated looking, with tiny little stores offering who knows what goods.

At one point we passed a vehicle boneyard where piles of

burned and shot-up tanks and other military equipment were stacked, remnants of the First Gulf War, the war my father fought. Lights from the highway eerily lit up the piles of vehicles where rust and desert sand couldn't mask the violence that had caused such destruction.

Despite the newness of the view outside my window, I was exhausted. It had been a long, emotional day, starting with the ceremony at the deployment center where we said farewell to our families. There had been speeches, lots of tears, lots of photo taking. A couple of television crews from different El Paso TV stations and print journalists from local newspapers had been there, interviewing people, asking hard questions.

My family had taken it all in stride, having seen it all so many times before. Nikki's deployments had already prepared them for saying good-bye to a daughter. My parents were so accustomed to soldier deployments that they said good-bye to me as if I were leaving on just another trip, just another stay away from home.

Long after my family left, my friend Theresa Rowland surprised me by showing up and crying as if she would never see me again.

"What are you crying about?" I asked her. "Six months will go by before you know it. Everything is going to be okay."

"I know," she said tearfully. "I'm just going to miss you so much."

I hugged her and tried to reassure her that I would be back. Her tears made it hard for me to stay dry eyed and I didn't want to cry in front of my daughter. Janelle would be with her grandparents and I knew she would be just fine, in familiar surroundings and perfectly cared for.

So it had been a long, emotional day by the time we arrived at Camp Virginia. The buses and trucks were stopped at the gates of the camp. Guards boarded each bus and we all fumbled around to dig out our ID cards. A soldier walked down the aisle of the bus, checking each card, his eyes bouncing from the picture to our faces one by one. Eventually we were allowed through the gate, and everyone was sitting up now as we all checked out the camp through the windows. We passed rows and rows of tents, Connex trailers, and low flat warehouse-looking buildings. The rows of tents seemed to go on forever. Eventually we stopped in an assembly area and were allowed to stumble off the bus. Somehow, after a time, I found my duffel bags in the mountain of green that was tossed down from the trucks.

There was a lot of milling about as everyone sorted out their things, figured out where their living area would be, who would be assigned to which tents. Of course, the women's tent wasn't anywhere near where our bags were dropped off, so it took a couple of trips of heavy hauling to get everything moved into the place I would call home for the duration of our stay.

The women were lucky. The tents could hold as many as fifteen people each, and since there were only nine of us, we could use empty cots to pile our stuff on and didn't have to leave our duffel bags lying on the floor. I knew the men would be shoulder to shoulder in their tents with little room to spare. My sleeping bag was at the bottom of one of my duffels, so I wrestled with getting it out of my bag along with my pillow and shower gear. I unrolled the sleeping bag on top of the cot, but as inviting as it looked, I wasn't quite ready to turn in.

"Where are the showers?" I couldn't go to bed until I had cleaned up a little. A couple of the other women joined me for our first of many trips to the showers.

We trudged down the road, past tent after tent, gravel crunching beneath our boots. There were a few people walking around, but most folks were already in their racks for the night. The roads were lit with soft yellow lights, the sounds of generators a constant rumble. The showers were in large Connex trailers that were fitted with proper sinks and individual shower stalls with plastic curtains and rubber mats on the floor. The water pressure wasn't great, but the showers were clean and the water was hot. It wasn't the Hilton but I had been in far worse places. It would do.

I had left my daughter and my family and gone off to war, but I spent my first night in the desert feeling so exhausted there was little time to think about it. Still, I knew I could handle it, I could get through the deployment just fine, and then I'd go home and eventually it would all be a distant memory. I knew we had lots of training to go through and that there were rumors I would have to move into Iraq along with the rest of my unit, but at the time, even the prospect of moving with the unit seemed like something I could easily take. I had no idea what challenges I still faced.

11

Going to Baghdad

Two men rode in the front seat, another in the backseat with me. I wished I'd been crammed in the back of the truck with the men. Even though my seat was more comfortable, I didn't want to be with these mean-looking guys who talked among themselves as if I wasn't there. They kept the windows open, and when we passed people on the road, they brandished their weapons and screamed something triumphant sounding, honking their horn and generally calling attention to themselves. They were proud of the prizes they were carrying.

The first group of men had stripped me of my chemical suit jacket and my uniform top. I wore only my brown T-shirt, and that seemed to offend the group of men I was with now. The man in the backseat draped a blanket across my shoulders as if my arms and the close-fitting T-shirt were too revealing.

"This is Iraq," he said, as if I had had a choice in my wardrobe and needed scolding.

I was still feeling the effects of the painkiller I had been given, and I seemed to float in and out of it, knowing where I was and what was going on but not feeling completely there. Despite the painkiller, I was aware of my wounds, aware of the throbbing in my legs. Fear became a minor distraction from the pain.

We pulled into a town and our captors continued to scream and yell out the windows, brandishing the M16 as if it were proof of their victory against the invaders. Eventually they gained the attention they were seeking and slowed to a halt as people started pouring out of buildings and gathering around the truck. Older men in traditional long robes and younger men in Western clothes surrounded the vehicle from all sides to see the captured Americans. The crowd, prompted by the guards, joined in the yelling and screaming and very quickly they grew in numbers until it was a fairly large mob. They were kicking up dust as they milled around the truck, getting worked up into a frenzy. Some were laughing and dancing, their arms raised in triumph. Most of them looked angry, like things could get ugly very quickly.

The man who had ridden in the backseat with me opened my door so the villagers could get a better look at me. I probably should have been worried that my captors were going to throw me to the mob, but the painkiller caused me to sort of watch it all happen, the door opening and the crowd getting excited, as if I were detached from the scene, completely oblivious to the danger. Suddenly, from out of nowhere, someone slapped me. He leaned into the open door and gave me a good smack across the face. That woke me up real quick. My head snapped back and, like the effects of the slap the doctor had given me earlier, I was suddenly very aware of what was going on around me. I could tell others in the crowd thought the blow was a good idea and wanted to get a whack at me themselves. I had already been slapped three times that day and three times was plenty. I wanted out of there.

Eventually the guards realized the joyous crowd they had

gathered was quickly turning into an uncontrollable mob. It took them long enough! Once they finally started seeing the madness and danger of the throng, they closed my door and fought their way back into the truck, and we left.

It was suddenly very quiet in the car as we careened back down the road. The guards mumbled back and forth to one another, and I can only assume they were commenting on how they barely got us out of there.

I have no idea how long we drove; the effects of the drug caused me to lose track of time, lose track of where we were. What I did know was that we were going to Baghdad. The entire trip, those times when I was lucid, I thought about Baghdad with such dread, such fear. I knew the possibility of torture was very real and the closer we got to the city, the more real that fear became.

But we weren't done stopping in towns yet. We weren't done getting shown off. Our arrival in each place was the scene of an excited mob, as if word had spread that we were coming. In the next town, my guards decided not to open the door for my display, they simply opened my window for the crowd to get a good look. I didn't get slapped this time, but someone spit on me.

I had never been spit on before. It was almost worse than the slap, to have that man's angry spittle on my face. I was grateful the guards hadn't opened the door this time, knowing these angry crowds had the potential to get much more violent than they had been so far. I had already been punched and kicked by an angry crowd once that day and I didn't want another scene like that.

There was too much going on for me to know what the guys were going through. I at least had my hands free and could wipe the spittle off my face. The men were bound and crowded together in the back of the truck. I wondered how they were.

We stopped in four different towns on our way to Baghdad.

Each time there was the shouting and horn honking as we drove in, crowds forming, more shouting and angry men surrounding our truck. In the next two towns, my guards didn't roll down the window, didn't open the door. It must have bothered them that I had been slapped and spit on. They seemed to be protecting me from further humiliation and I wondered about that. I was grateful, but I wondered why they had made the accommodation.

In between towns there was little in the way of buildings or people. The closer we got to Baghdad, however, the more trees there were, the more patches of grass and vegetation. Eventually the road started to look more like a highway. It divided into four lanes with large green directional signs and a concrete meridian that had been planted with flowers and grasses. We were getting closer to the city.

We made a few turns and entered a series of city streets and it was obvious we had arrived in Baghdad. Dull brown shops lined the road and there were more people on the sidewalks and more traffic in the streets. The driver wasn't honking the horn now. I wondered why they had decided not to publicize who they had in the truck. I wondered about it, but I was relieved. The village crowds had been ugly and frightening. I could only imagine how badly a Baghdad mob would react to American POWs in their grasp.

The guards weren't trying to get attention from the people on the street but they were doing a lot of talking among themselves. Finally, the driver stopped and waved some random guy over to the truck. I realized he was asking directions! These guys had no idea where to go. It surprised me. I started to wonder who these guys were and why it had fallen to them to bring us to the big city.

Several times they stopped and were directed on a different course and finally one guy actually crowded into the front seat of the truck to show them which way to go. He directed us to a set of buildings inside a gated courtyard where several Iraqi men in uniform were standing around. The men were unloaded from the back of the truck and were given water. The guards left me alone in the truck while everyone was sort of standing around waiting for our escorts to figure out what to do next.

One of the Iraqi soldiers wandered over to me and asked, *"Sprechen sie Deutsch?"*

"Nein," I said, conjuring up the little German I did know. *"Ich spreche kein Deutsch."* The man wandered away.

I watched as the guys were all escorted into one of the buildings and the Iraqi soldiers who had been standing around went inside, too. I was left alone outside in the truck. I figured they had all decided I wasn't going anywhere on my shot-up legs and they were right. I wasn't going to get far if I took off. A wounded black woman in uniform wandering around Baghdad wasn't going to last long, so I stayed put. But I did figure this might be my only opportunity to get rid of my notebook with all of the radio call signs and grid coordinates. I thought about what to do. My hands weren't tied, so I tried to pull up a small segment of carpet on the floor of the truck near my feet. It was an older truck, so the carpet near the door was a bit loose. I was afraid of getting caught, afraid someone would come out to check on me before I got the job done. I kept my eye on the building and tugged at the carpet until it came up and a section of the metal frame was exposed. I rolled up the small notebook and shoved it down into one of the holes in the exposed metal frame. It was a tight fit, but I managed to get the whole thing down there and patted the carpet back into place with my bare foot.

My heart was thudding in my chest when I was finished. I had gotten rid of the notebook but it wasn't the best hiding place.

I hoped I could get out of that truck without anyone discovering what I had done to the carpet. I kept pressing my foot down on it to make sure it wouldn't pop up again and worried about what would happen if the notebook was found.

Eventually the men were escorted out of the building and instructed to sit down near a large planter in the courtyard. One of the guards came over to get me. He took my arm and tried to support me as I hobbled over to where the men were. Every step was torture. By the time I was seated near the guys, I was breathless and woozy with the pain. We were given water and we waited. The Iraqis took pictures of us and someone brought out a video camera. They didn't ask us any questions. They each wanted personal photos for their scrapbooks of the American captives. It was surprising that they didn't put themselves in the pictures, like tourists standing next to a celebrity. "Hey, take a picture of me with the American POWs!" After a time, we were loaded back into the truck and taken to yet another location.

This time, when we pulled into the courtyard, it was clear we were arriving in a place that was different, a place where our captivity began to seem more real. Armed men in uniform with serious expressions surrounded the truck, unloaded us, and escorted us inside. They seemed so serious, in fact, that I decided I had better do my best to walk.

I stepped gingerly out of the truck and followed the men. There is no way to describe how painful those steps were. The pain of my bare feet pressed into the tiny gravel courtyard was barely noticeable. My legs felt shattered beneath me, but I walked, hobbled along as best I could. I was petrified that carrying me would quickly become too much of a burden. The more of a burden I was, the more likely it was that they would tire of me, and if they tired of me, they could just take me out and shoot me. That's what was going through my head anyway, when I sucked up the pain and carried myself on my devastated legs.

The three men who had taken us this far stepped back as if they had handed us over to a new set of handlers. The new guards ushered us into a room and it was immediately clear who was in charge. He was a stern-looking officer with a thick mustache, straight in bearing and serious looking. They roughly instructed us to empty our pockets. I stood there, in so much pain with my legs barely supporting me, silently thanking God that I had hidden that damn notebook when I had had the opportunity. All I had left in my pockets was some of the precious toilet paper I had been rationing out to myself, hoping to make it last as long as possible. Now that small luxury would be gone. After our pockets were emptied, they instructed Miller and Riley to remove their glasses. I knew neither of them would be happy about losing the ability to see clearly.

One man spoke English, but he seemed to be translating what the officer in charge instructed him to say. "If you do as you are told, you will be okay," he said. "If you do not, you will be shot."

The way these guys looked, I had no doubt they would do what they had threatened. I decided I would follow their instructions to the letter, if I could. Then, for the first time, my hands were tied. The men had been tied before, but I hadn't been and I didn't like the feeling. I was watching closely as the soldiers went around the room to tie us up and blindfold us. One soldier, not liking the way I was watching everything, used the barrel of his AK-47 to push my head down so that my eyes were lowered.

Something about the way he forced my head down pissed me off. I was standing there on my shot-up legs, my hands tied, surrounded by men with weapons. What difference could it make if I watched what was going on? And it wasn't like we hadn't already had a good look at all of them. I didn't have much time to feel angry about it before they blindfolded me.

Yet again, we were taken outside to be loaded into the back of a different truck. Every step was a new level of agony, but I was afraid for my life. I wasn't about to ask these guys to carry me. It was easy to see that these guys wouldn't have had any patience for my issues. I walked.

We were loaded onto bench seats facing the center. The blindfold and having my hands tied made this trip much different from the others. I didn't know who was sitting next to me. I thought it was an Iraqi soldier but I didn't know for sure. I knew there were plenty of others in the vehicle, but I couldn't tell whether all the men had gotten into the truck with me. I feared I was now traveling alone with the Iraqi soldiers. There was no way to tell. The blindfold, the motion of the truck through the streets, were all disorienting and just plain scary.

When we finally arrived at our new destination, I again tried my best to walk on my own. I was in excruciating pain, and my feet were not accustomed to being without shoes. I was petrified. So I walked and tried not to moan.

I was led into the building, down a hallway, into a room, and pushed onto a chair. My hands were untied and my blindfold was removed. One man sat at a table to my right, a notebook in front of him as if he were ready to record what happened next. He looked European, with blond hair and blue eyes. Two men in Iraqi uniforms sat on either side of me. They frightened me. They watched my every movement. I looked at them, my head swiveling back and forth, wondering why they were sitting there. Two other men, one of them wearing a long dark robe and a dark-colored turban, paced around the room like predators circling their prey. There were two men with video cameras in the room, both cameras trained on me.

If their intention was to look intimidating, to make me nervous, to frighten the crap out of me, they succeeded. They all watched me with serious expressions and it was obvious that my interrogation was about to begin.

12

Prayers

We celebrated Good Friday in Kuwait with a service in the chapel tent on Camp Virginia. Pie and I and several other Catholics in the unit attended the mass, taking Communion, singing hymns, just sharing in the service. I don't go to mass every Sunday, but while in Kuwait we all probably went to services more than usual.

We knew we would be leaving on our convoy soon and just about anyone who was a churchgoer was there that day. Soldiers were lined up along the walls and most seats were filled. I knew it could be a while before I was able to go to mass again, so I actively listened, paid attention to everything that was said. Maybe that's why what the chaplain said stuck with me.

"We are a highly technical military. We are well equipped and advanced," he prayed. "But we know that nothing can be done without Your presence and without Your guidance."

That struck me as being very true at the time, and as we prepared to go on the convoy, to who knew where, I thought about that prayer. After the prayer and just before the end of the service, we sang "Amazing Grace." It's one of those old standards you hear all the time, but after that service the song really stuck in my head. We still had days of preparation before we would head out, and the song was always kind of there at the back of my mind.

We spent a month at Camp Virginia and much of it was spent waiting—waiting to pick up equipment, waiting to take classes, waiting to see what would happen next. You couldn't travel off base unless you were in a convoy, so one of the first things we learned was how to conduct convoy operations. No matter where we ended up, we would need to be on the road picking up equipment and supplies, so we needed to become experts in proper convoy procedures, specifically how to pull security while in a convoy. To pull security, we were to get out of the truck; the driver and passenger were to go to opposite ends of the vehicle; we had to have our weapons at the ready and eyes open for anyone or anything suspicious coming toward us. We were still in Kuwait, so the likelihood of anyone attacking us while on the road was remote, but we wouldn't be in Kuwait forever. We needed to be aware of every possible danger, no matter where we might end up next.

Sergeant Riley taught a class about land mines, how to identify them, what to do if you found one, where to look for them. Riley had some specialized training in the subject and he seemed confident as he stood in front of the class delivering the lecture. He had examples of a variety of mines displayed on a table and it was obvious that he had spent a lot of time preparing for the class. He explained that the bad guys might booby-trap something appealing, something that might make you feel curious and want to check it out, so that you'd pick it up and detonate the explosive. It was a trick used by insurgents in conflicts past and there was no reason to assume the tactic wouldn't be used on us.

"Bottom line is, if you see something on the ground, no matter what it is, don't pick it up," he said. "Even if it's shiny and pretty, don't start thinking you could use it to make a nice pair of earrings."

Most of the people in the class chuckled a little bit, but I didn't think it was funny. "Hold on now," I said, piping up. "What do you mean, make some earrings out of it?"

"Oh, you know what I mean," Riley said, turning a little red.

"No, I don't know what you mean. That sounds a little sexist to me. Like you think women will just bend down and pick up anything that's shiny so we can make some daggone earrings out of it."

Well, he didn't know what to say to that. Some of the men grumbled like I was making a big deal out of nothing, but some of the women in the room were nodding, agreeing with me but not jumping into the argument.

Sergeant Riley shrugged it all off and moved on with the class and I had to just chalk up the comment as just another way of saying women didn't have a role to play in a war. Here I was, about to go into a war zone, with the men sitting around me in that room, and I still wasn't getting the respect as a soldier they gave each other.

After being in Kuwait about ten days, we were sent to pick up our trucks at the port. We had flown to Kuwait, and the rest of our equipment arrived on a large cargo ship. We had to travel to the port, pick up the equipment, and bring it back to Camp Virginia. We were each assigned to be part of a team of two, then assigned a truck to pick up and drive back.

First Sergeant Dowdy had been assigned to the 507th late and didn't join us in Kuwait until after we had already been there for some time. He came to us as our new first sergeant, not having trained with us at Fort Bliss or been with us during the deployment preparation or even flown with us to this desert location.

Our training had made us a tight-knit team and some of us, me included, weren't too happy to be assigned a brand-new first sergeant just days before we were supposed to head into a conflict.

Dowdy was a textbook first sergeant, over six feet tall with a crew cut, a muscular build, a perfect uniform, and the stern expression that went along with his rank. He was a no-nonsense kind of first sergeant who didn't have patience for excuses or time to be friendly about it. I didn't like him much, but there's a reason why first sergeants are so stern. They are the highest-ranking non-commissioned officers in the company, the guys responsible for training and preparation of everyone in their unit. It must be an awesome responsibility. I didn't like Dowdy when he first arrived, but I grew to appreciate his professionalism and to trust him. When the bullets started flying, it was Dowdy I trusted to come back for us, to stick with us, and he did, and it cost him his life.

Picking up our vehicles, around sixty big trucks and Humvees, was the first large task he would have to lead us through. He had his work cut out for him.

Dowdy gave us a safety briefing before we left. There were a lot of ways this mission could go wrong. We could have breakdowns on the road, get into accidents with locals who might not be too happy about us on their roads, or we could run into Iraqi infiltrators coming over the border to cause trouble.

In anticipation of running into serious trouble like that, we were all issued a magazine of live rounds for our M16s. It was the first time, outside of a firing range, I had ever been issued live ammunition. Carrying an M16 was second nature, something I was accustomed to. Carrying an M16 along with bullets meant I had not only a weapon but the means to actually kill someone in my hands. It was unsettling. I had fired live rounds on weapons ranges before, but I was shooting at paper or pop-up targets. We were now in a war zone and we had live rounds. It didn't take a huge mental leap to realize that we might have to actually point the business end of our weapon at someone and pull the trigger. I have to say, I took some long moments to think about that. Could I do it? Could I kill someone? If it came to them or me, if it came to them or one of the people in my unit, you're damn straight I could do it. It was disturbing to think about killing someone, but I knew I wouldn't hesitate if it came down to it.

They issued us the live rounds, which we loaded into thirty-round magazines. Then they told us to cover the hole in the magazine with tape. Each magazine has a small hole in the side. I'm not sure what the purpose of the hole is, but it does give you a quick visual that there are rounds in the magazine. We were told to use what we call hundred-mile-an-hour tape, a thick green tape with a heavy sticky back, to wrap the entire magazine, including the hole. Folks in the Army use hundred-mile-an-hour tape like civilians use duct tape. We use it to silence things that can clang, to hold extra straps in place, and, now, to cover the holes in our magazines.

I didn't understand why we were told to use the tape on our magazines. Maybe they thought it would protect the magazines from desert sand. I had never heard of the practice before, and when I walked around our base camp in Kuwait, I didn't see any other soldiers outside the 507th with the stripe of tape on their magazines, but like everyone else, I followed the orders as they were given. Later, I would question if that tape didn't contribute to the disaster we would soon face.

Our instructions were that if we should break down on the trip back from the port or get into an accident, we were to stay with our vehicle, wait for someone from the unit to come back and help us, and pull security until help arrived.

I was assigned to ride with Corporal Damien Luten, and of course, of all the vehicles that had to be picked up, I had to get the one that would break down. We had been on the road for about an hour when the thing started coughing and sputtering and we didn't have any choice but to pull over to the side of the road. We sat in the cab of the truck cursing for a moment, before we both climbed down from the cab to pull security. We went to our respective ends of the truck, him up front and me around to the rear, and watched as cars and small trucks flew by us on the highway. Others in our unit had seen us pulling over to the side, so we knew that if we waited it out, someone would be along to help us out.

Eventually a Kuwaiti police car pulled over. The young police officers got out of their vehicle and tentatively sauntered over to us. Luten said hello. They said hello back but that was about the extent of their English. One of them offered us cigarettes, which we both declined. We stood around awkwardly, communication impossible, when one of them offered us something to eat. They looked like small cakes, a sticky vanilla-looking pound cake with some kind of fruitlike filling. They looked a little like Twinkies. We had been instructed not to eat food offered to us by the locals for fear they would try to drug or poison us or something equally paranoid. But these two seemed completely innocent of such a deception. Luten took one look at the offer and said, "Yes, *snacks*," and eagerly gobbled up the sweet cake. I didn't try the cake but I appreciated the gesture.

It was my first time outside the gates of the camp since we had arrived and my first time seeing everything in daylight. The desert is flat and brown and more rock than sand. The highway we were on was just a straight and flat four-lane road that was used by a steady stream of traffic. The cars on the road were everything from rattling junkers to shiny new luxury sedans. Some cars had curtains over the backseat and rear windows and I knew women were hidden behind them. It was hot, hotter than Fort Bliss even, which can get extremely hot, but we had plenty of water and some MREs, so we simply waited. It was over two hours before someone finally came to tow us back to camp and the policemen waited with us the whole time; I thought that was nice of them. We said good-bye to the Kuwaiti policemen and left.

Once the United States started bombing Baghdad, rumors quickly spread that we would be moving up into the heart of Iraq along with most of the combat units assembled in Kuwait. First Sergeant Dowdy kept telling us that we would be going into Iraq, but I brushed off the news, filing it under the I'll-believe-it-when-it-happens file of the many things I had heard through the rumor mill since we had arrived. Then, just three days after the war had started in earnest, Captain King confirmed the rumors. In our usual morning formation, our unit assembled in neat rows and stood at attention; First Sergeant Dowdy turned the company over to Captain King, who told us we would be making a movement and we should be prepared as soon as the word came down. We would be convoying into Iraq to set up camp at a place to be determined. He told us that we should be prepared to be on the road for several days and to have adequate supplies for the trip.

When I remembered to breathe again, I was resigned to do what was necessary but scared to death as well. I had been over the logic in my head so many times I had managed to convince myself we would stay put. Even though we were in the desert, even though bombs were dropping on Baghdad, I simply knew I would remain far away from combat. I didn't understand what role I could possibly play in this fight. I didn't understand why supply specialists and maintainers and cooks should have to leave the base camp to go into Iraq. I didn't understand what the Army was thinking and I still don't. I kept thinking that at some point, someone would figure out I wasn't needed in the heart of Iraq, but that never happened.

On March 20, 2003, the line of trucks that pulled out of the camp snaked for miles throughout Camp Virginia. The 507th was at the rear of the convoy of over six hundred trucks. The impossibly long line of vehicles would take hours to weave its way out of the camp gates.

A military convoy is like a planned traffic jam. You simply have to prepare yourself to wait, to move slowly, to know that no amount of maneuvering will help. The order of march determines your place in line. You're stuck in it. The rear of the truck in front of you is what you will be looking at for hours on end. You will try to maintain a good distance between your vehicle and the one in front of you, but there will be times when you'll get too close, fall too far behind, or simply stop for no apparent reason.

I didn't know Hernandez that well when I climbed into his truck. He was a quiet guy and I hadn't talked to him much up to that point, but we would be in that vehicle for days and I figured we would have plenty of time to get to know each other.

The day hadn't started well for me. Somehow that morning I had cut my hand on my M16. I couldn't figure out how I had cut it—it wasn't like there were any sharp edges on the weapon. I took that cut, and the strangeness of it happening, as a sign of bad luck and it wasn't long before I was proven right.

Almost as soon as Hernandez and I made it out of the gate, we heard the long blast of a horn, followed quickly by voices from several trucks screaming, "Gas, gas, gas! Go to MOPP level four."

"Oh my God!" I said. "We just got out of the gate! How can this be happening so soon?"

MOPP 4 (mission-oriented protective posture) is the highest level of preparation for a chemical attack. We had to immediately pull over and put on our chemical suits, rubber boots, long thick rubber gloves, and chemical masks. My hands were shaking as I worked to put on the cumbersome equipment. A chemical suit is hot in most circumstances. In that desert heat it was positively de-bilitating. The hood of the mask, the rubber gloves, and the thick charcoal-lined suit were not meant to be worn in hundred-degree heat. I had to believe that attack was real if someone was going to order us to wear the equipment. Once we were properly suited up, the convoy started moving again. Somehow Hernandez was driving that big truck while looking through the thick plastic of his uncomfortable mask.

We drove for a while like that, baking like trussed turkeys in the oven-hot suits, hearing our Darth Vader–like breath wheez-ing in and out of the rubber mask. A short time later, thank goodness, we were told to remove the mask but to keep wearing the suit until told otherwise. We gratefully removed the masks, took off the gloves and boots, and wore the chemical suit jackets unzipped. The immediate relief from removing the gear was short-lived, however. We were driving in hundred-degree heat and the extra-thick layer of clothing wasn't helping, but Hernan-dez and I wore those hot suits the entire convoy trip and were wearing them when we were captured. Chemical protection suits are lined in charcoal, a thick black layer that is supposed to pro-tect you from skin irritants and other nasty things the enemy can throw at you.

The charcoal lining of the suits would later become a painful problem for both Hernandez and me.

For three days we drove with little sleep and infrequent breaks. We drove where everyone else drove and turned when everyone else turned. When other trucks broke down, we got out of our truck, pulled security, and helped out however we could. Neither one of us had any idea where we were going, and as it turns out, that was probably a good thing.

The

ARMY CODE
of CONDUCT

★

I am an American fighting in the forces that guard my country and our way of life. I am prepared to give my life in their defense.

I will never surrender of my own free will. If in command, I will never surrender the members of my command while they still have the means to resist.

If I am captured I will continue to resist by all means available. I will make every effort to escape and aid others to escape. I will accept neither parole nor special favors from the enemy.

If I become a prisoner of war, I will keep faith with my fellow prisoners. I will give no information or take part in any action which might be harmful to my comrades. If I am senior, I will take command. If not, I will obey the lawful orders of those appointed over me and will back them up in every way.

Should I become a prisoner of war, I am required to give name, rank, service number, and date of birth. I will evade answering further questions to the utmost of my ability. I will make no oral or written statements disloyal to my country and its allies.

I will never forget that I am an American fighting for freedom, responsible for my actions, and dedicated to the principles which made my country free. I will trust in my God and in the United States of America.

13

Interrogation

I was fully alert now; all of the effects of the pain medication I had taken earlier had worn off. I didn't know what I could or couldn't tell the interrogators and maybe that made my answers sound cagey. I wasn't trying to be clever. I wasn't holding any secrets. I simply didn't know anything of strategic value to them. They all sat staring at me and looking like my worst nightmare. The blond spoke perfect English. He asked the questions and did the translating. Most of my answers were easy. I simply said I didn't know.

Then he asked, "How far into Kuwait is your camp?"

Our bases in Kuwait had been there since we had liberated that country from Iraq during the First Gulf War. What were they asking me that for?

I said, "About thirty klicks."

They looked at each other and exchanged a few words. Finally the blond asked, "How far is a klick?"

Klick is an Army term for "kilometer." I could have told them it was a kilometer, I guess, but I played dumb. "About one-point-two miles," I said, wide-eyed and scared. They either really didn't know what a klick was or figured I wasn't going to be any more forthcoming. I knew a kilometer was less than a mile long, but I just played dumb. The questions got harder, but there was nothing I could tell them.

"I'm just a cook," I told them. "I don't know anything."

Their expressions told me that I hadn't convinced them of my insignificance. Surely they had to know that we had only fallen into the ambush because we had been lost, had stumbled into the wrong place at the wrong time. Surely they knew that we had been at the tail end of a six-hundred-vehicle convoy. How important could we have been if we had been left behind in such a huge group of trucks?

"You say you've been in the Army several years, but you don't know the answers to these questions?" the blond man asked.

"They don't tell me anything," I said.

"Why don't they tell you anything?" he asked yet again.

"They don't tell me these things in case something like this happens."

They kept at it for over an hour. I had no idea what time it was, but it was late in the evening. I expected the interrogation to get worse as time went on. I didn't know how well I could handle it. We had been on the road for three days with almost no sleep when we were attacked and that had been in the predawn hours of a day that seemed never-ending. I was done. Finished. Used up. I sat there looking at those men, expecting the worst—torture, at least a beating—but it never happened.

"Do you need anything?" the blond asked.

"I need a doctor to look at my legs," I said.

"Okay," he said, and finally they seemed through with me. One of the Iraqi soldiers tied my hands again and put the blindfold back on. He led me from the room, shuffling on my sore legs. I took a minute to feel some relief that the interrogation was over, but I knew that fact could be temporary. The guard led me into a room and sat me down on the floor. I could hear that there were other people; the slight rustling of clothing let me know that the rest of the men were in the room. I was relieved by that knowledge. The guard took someone else out and I figured it was their turn to face the questions.

We sat there like that, silent, our hands tied and blindfolded as each of us was taken out and questioned. A man came in and told me he was a doctor. With my blindfold still on, he offered me more painkillers. I refused them.

"Oh, you are strong woman," he said.

I wasn't trying to be strong. The last painkiller they had given me was so powerful it had me feeling groggy and out of it. We were in Baghdad now and I didn't want to risk not being fully aware of what was going on. I didn't want to be stupid. So I turned down the painkiller. I almost regretted not taking it when he unwrapped the bandages on my legs to clean the wounds. Maybe it was because I couldn't see what he was doing, but it hurt like hell. It took all of my strength not to scream in agony. I fought through the pain and pictured the raw meat and ragged edges of my flesh I had seen when the doctor treated my wounds earlier. I knew walking around wasn't helping. I was pretty sure there was broken bone in my left leg and both of my feet were so swollen it was hard to recognize them as belonging to me. As horrible as the pain was, I vowed I wouldn't take any more of the painkillers. I needed to be alert, and if nothing else, the pain kept me present. Eventually he redid all of the bandages and gave me antibiotics.

When the doctor left, someone came around with water, pressing the glass to my lips, trying to get me to drink. Then he forced figs into my mouth, pushing them between my lips until I had to eat them. I felt helpless and disgusted by the force-feeding. I don't know how long we sat in that room but it seemed like hours of anxiety, wondering what would happen next. At some point, I heard someone snoring. Snoring! As exhausted as I was, I couldn't believe anyone could sleep under those conditions. I learned later that it was Miller who was sleeping. Exhaustion is the only possible explanation.

Finally they came in and stood each of us up. We were shuffled down the hall and I was loaded back into a truck. I had lost track of the sounds and couldn't tell if all the men had been loaded in the truck along with me. I could tell that I was sitting between two Iraqi guards and I worried again that I might have been separated from the rest of the men.

I was jolted around between the two guards as we drove the city streets. The vehicle stopped and there was lots of shouting, similar-sounding to what I had heard when we had made stops in the villages on the way to Baghdad. There were triumphant chants and the raised voices of scores of angry men. Then I was almost knocked off my seat as the truck began a violent rocking motion. Back and forth we rocked as the mob surrounded us and pushed the vehicle from side to side. The guards on either side of me laughed and shouted, getting caught up in the excitement of the crowd. The rocking and shouting seemed endless. We stopped at least three more times on our way to our destination as the guards took advantage of our presence to make a triumphant tour of the city. I wondered what they said in the chants. Death to American soldiers? Down with America? There was no way to tell exactly what was said, but the sentiment was very clear. If that mob could have gotten their hands on me, I would have been torn to pieces.

Eventually, we arrived at our destination. We pulled up

somewhere that sounded as if we had entered yet another courtyard; the street noises seemed distant and muffled. Rough hands
grabbed me by the arm and stood me up outside the truck. The
pain in my legs was unbearable but I forced myself to walk, choking back moans as we moved into the building.

I was led into a room that sounded and felt small. My hands
were untied and my blindfold was removed. There were two
guards in the room with me, both of them armed, both of them
young and serious looking. They left me standing there and closed
the door.

As soon as the door clanged shut, the room was plunged into
total darkness. I couldn't see a thing. My brief glimpse of my surroundings made me think I was in a prison cell. As if to confirm, I
heard a hard metallic click as the thick metal door was locked from
the other side. The cell was short and narrow. As my eyes adjusted
to the darkness I could see there was a narrow opening with prison
bars high up on the wall opposite the door.

It was too dark. I had to fight back a moment of panic. After all
of the moving around, all of the changes throughout the day, it felt
as if I had been shoved in too abruptly and I didn't want to be left
here like this. Suddenly the door opened again and I almost sighed
in relief.

Two guards came in with Miller in tow. I was relieved to see
Miller. At least now I knew that I wasn't at this prison alone. One
of the guards handed me a set of neatly folded clothing.

"Change," he said, shoving the pile of clothes at me.

I glanced at Miller, then back at the guard, and just shook my
head. "I'm not changing in front of you," I said.

He repeated himself, more forceful this time. "Change," he
demanded.

Miller turned his head toward the wall, as if I had little choice but to follow the instructions. There was no way I was doing that. I shook my head again. "No," I said.

The guards exchanged a few words and then one of them left, looking frustrated. I stood my ground and waited to see what would happen next. The man returned carrying a blanket. He held it up high as a shield between myself and the men. I took a moment to feel slightly triumphant, then took the pile of clothes and began to change.

They were like cheap men's cotton pajamas with faded pink and white stripes. On the pocket of the pajamas were the letters *PW*, which I assumed meant prisoner of war. I was grateful for the cheap, clear gray plastic sandals that completed the ensemble. I took off my uniform pants and put on the new bottoms, which hung long and loose on me. I had already lost my uniform top when we had first been captured, so all I was wearing was my sports bra and brown Army T-shirt. I kept the T-shirt on, put the pajama top on over it, and gingerly slipped my swollen feet into the plastic sandals. I gathered my uniform, the legs all torn and bloody, into a bundle.

"Okay," I said.

I handed my pile of clothing to the guard who had been holding the blanket, then, with a final glance at Miller, I was led out of the cell. We stepped into the hallway and my impression that we were in a prison was confirmed. The hall was lined with cell doors, each with a metal window for guards to keep watch. We moved at a snail's pace down the hallway; the guards accommodated my wounds by matching the speed of my shuffle. We passed several doors and ended up facing a cell door on the other side of the hall.

I stepped inside and took a good look at the room. It looked clean and stark. The walls were a light bluish-looking brick with a gray cement floor. I didn't see any rodents or bugs and I was relieved at that. A guard handed me a bedroll. I untied the bundle and spread it out. I sat down on the thin mattress ticking and wondered how long I would have to live like this.

An official-looking soldier came in and asked my name, writing it down in a large book. There was something comforting in knowing that a record would be kept of me, that even if I disappeared tomorrow, my name had been written down somewhere as if I had carved *Shoshana Johnson was here, 2003,* like graffiti on the walls.

Someone brought me a plate of crackers and cheese. It seemed like hours since I had eaten last. The plain saltine crackers were tasteless but helped to calm my stomach. Eventually, they closed my door again. I lay in the pitch-darkness, listening to the noises of the prison, running through all that had happened that day, my first day in captivity, fearful that I would never sleep. I closed my eyes.

When I opened them again, light was streaming in through the small window high up in the wall.

14

New Places

Considering that I was raised an Army brat, my family really didn't move that many times. We moved from Panama to California when I was five. My dad, a fireman when we lived in Panama, joined the Army shortly after we arrived in the States. My mom, sisters, and I stayed in California while he went to basic training and AIT (advanced individual training). We were left in the familiar surroundings of Los Angeles, where our aunts and uncles and a bunch of cousins lived, while he completed his training. We eventually moved with Dad to Fort Lewis, Washington, for a couple of years. When my dad was ordered to Germany for the first time, his orders didn't allow him to bring his family, so we moved back to Los Angeles to be near the family while he was away. After his Germany tour, we all made the move for a brief stay in Fort Carson, Colorado, and then we were ordered to Fort Bliss, Texas. Fort Bliss and the El Paso area have always felt like home since it was there that we spent most of our time.

I was going to elementary school near Fort Bliss when Dad received orders sending him back to Germany, only this time he was allowed to take his family. My sisters and I did not want to go. I had made the mistake of feeling like I could put down roots. I had lots of friends and a good routine at school, I was getting good grades and I liked our life there. I couldn't begin to imagine leaving all of that, let alone consider living in a place so far away. There was all kinds of drama over the announcement. Between my sisters and me, we shed lots of tears and we argued to stay, but despite all of our protests, we packed up and moved to Aschaffenburg, Germany.

My sisters and I look back on our time in Germany now and realize how great it was. My dad would leave in the predawn hours to go to PT with his unit on base. On his way home, he would stop at a bakery and bring home freshly baked *Brötchen,* the German bread rolls that come in all kinds of varieties, sometimes with cheese packed in the hard crust or cranberries, cinnamon, raisins, or nuts buried in the soft, tasty center. Dad would always bring us the plain bread but it would still be warm from the oven when we had it for breakfast. We would look forward to it again as an afternoon snack while doing our homework.

My parents had always been strict disciplinarians, keeping very close tabs on us, always keeping track of our movements, never giving us space to do what we pleased. It was different in Germany. They seemed more relaxed with us and we had more freedom than we had ever had before. Maybe it was because there was so little crime there, or maybe it was because they wanted us to experience more. Whatever the reason, we had more freedom and we took advantage of it.

I was twelve years old when we arrived. We lived just off base in military housing and walked to school from there, going back on base to attend the DODDS (Department of Defense Dependent School) junior high school. One thing about going to

DODDS schools is that new kids don't have the same stigma as they do in other school systems. There are always new kids coming and kids leaving. Friends are made quickly because you never know when someone's parent will need to pack up the family and leave.

Despite my fears of leaving all that was familiar behind in Texas, I quickly formed a new tight-knit group of friends to hang out with. We went to movies, shopped, and toured around. I had babysitting jobs and always worked a summer hire job on base. I earned some of my own money for the first time and that meant I could go shopping with my friends in town without adult supervision, something that would have been unheard of while living in Texas.

The kids I hung out with were a mixed bunch. White kids, black kids, girls and boys. Skin color had little if any influence on who we spent our time with. Music tastes, hobbies, and other interests weighed more heavily in our choices of friends.

My freshman year in high school I had two very good friends, Shannon Cornelius and Yvonne Lattimer. We hung out together a lot, doing our homework, listening to music, or shopping and walking through town. We were kind of an odd group, three black girls who liked to listen to rock and roll like Poison, Guns N' Roses, and other rock bands. We liked the Fresh Prince and LL Cool J and other hip-hop groups, but Guns N' Roses was our favorite band. We didn't let stereotypes or peer pressure govern what we liked or didn't like. We were independent and we tended to have the same dreams. Shannon joined the Army, too, and already has over seventeen years in uniform. She has deployed to Iraq at least twice and could end up going back again. I worry about her, but I often think about those days in Germany and how independent we were.

I suffered through my first crushes while in Germany. First it was Chad Lewis, then Roosevelt White, both black kids who somehow caught my eye. Roosevelt was such a beautiful dark chocolate kid that I couldn't take my eyes off him. Neither one of them knew I was alive. I would watch them from a distance and pine for them, but they never looked my way. I eventually got over them.

Then one day Ryan Bishop said one of those things that boys say when they want to make conversation but it comes out all wrong.

"You'll never get asked on a date with that big zit on your face," he kidded me.

I was already embarrassed by the new pimple, but he was being sweet, picking on me as a way to make conversation. Two weeks later, he asked me if I would go to the movies with him. He was blond haired and blue eyed and I liked his freckles. We were both on the honor roll and I liked the way he paid attention to me and made me laugh. I was thirteen years old.

Of course it only lasted a couple of weeks, but that first boy-friend kind of set the tone for all the men in my life. Not that it was any real conscious decision, but I've simply tended to date white men. It's never really been about looks, but more about how men make me feel. Since looks were never the highest thing on my priority list, color barely ever registered as a positive or negative for the men I've dated. My daughter's father is white and the man I call the Irishman, the man who stole my heart, the man I kept going back to over and over again, is also white, but their color had little to do with what attracted me in the first place.

So while I resisted going to Germany, it turned out to be a place where I made lasting friendships and where I first had an opportunity to be independent. I was raised in a family where the women strongly believed that a woman had to stand on her own two feet and not depend on men for everything.

While my sisters and I had more freedom than we'd ever had before, our parents still kept an eye on us and constantly reminded us to be on our best behavior. My final year in Germany, I was enrolled in the DODDS high school in Hanau. For some reason, there were a lot of girls in that school who became pregnant, fifteen- and sixteen-year-old high school students who were having babies sooner than they should.

Our mother had already covered all the facts of life with us but she took the opportunity to reiterate her feelings on the subject. "As a young lady, it is not proper to have sex until you are grown up and have finished your education," she instructed us as my sisters and I sat around the dining-room table. "Those young girls that are pregnant, what are they going to do? They won't have an education. They will have to depend on their parents for everything. How are they going to take care of themselves? You girls are smarter than that."

My father was more up-front about the issue. "No screwing," he said.

"Daddy!" we all cried, shocked by his frank speech.

"I said it plainly so there won't be any mistake about what I mean," he said.

By the time my own daughter was born, I wasn't married and I hadn't finished my education, but I was ready to take care of my baby. I was earning a good living and had the start of a good career. I was a soldier. I never would have guessed that my care for Janelle would be interrupted by becoming a prisoner of war. Who could have predicted such a thing?

15

Red Crescent

I woke up, that first morning in my cell, wondering if my family had already heard about what happened to my convoy. I wondered how they would be told, wondered how the event would be covered in the news. I worried about them, about my daughter, about my father and his delicate heart and what this news might do to him.

Faint sunlight through the small window at the end of the room soaked up the shadows in the corners of the small cell. The cell had seemed larger, more threatening, in the darkness. The daylight made it easier to take and I prayed I wouldn't be there long. It was hard not to think about rescue. Was anyone looking for us?

I knew Miller was in the prison with me but wasn't sure where the other men were. If we were all together, I thought, we would be easier to find. I feared that if I were alone, even with only Miller along, our presence might be much easier to hide.

My CamelBak, the backpack with a large water bottle inside, had been stolen from the truck along with all my other stuff after the ambush. I missed it the most since that's where I had shoved my rosary before we left. I remembered seeing it sitting at the top of the bag, and that first morning in my cell, I wished for it. I prayed anyway. It was the first of many long conversations I would have with God while sitting in my cell. That morning, I prayed for strength, for the people who hadn't made it, for my family.

My face and arms were covered in mosquito bites. The window openings high up on my cell walls were uncovered, allowing easy entry for any flying insect that wanted in. Mosquitoes wanted in and any exposed flesh was proof of that. I must have slept hard because the bites hadn't bothered my sleep at all, but they were sure evident on my exposed skin. I could feel that my face was covered in bug bites.

I had only been awake a short while when someone opened the cell door. I sat up on my mattress on the floor as two men came in, one carrying a medical bag. The middle-aged man with the bag was wearing glasses and a dark suit and sported a thick mustache. He introduced himself. "I am a doctor," he said. "I will take care of you." The doctor was assisted by a stocky man in uniform, who unsmilingly followed the doctor's instructions as if he were serving as a nurse.

The doctor's English was very good and he talked to me as he cleaned my wounds and changed my bandages, which were soaked through. The bottom of my pajama pant legs were stiff with dried blood. There wasn't much change in the way my legs looked. My feet were still swollen and the gaping wounds still looked like raw and ravaged meat. The wound on my right calf was huge and gory looking. I worried about infection and wondered why the bleeding continued to seep so continuously through my bandages. The throbbing pain was becoming a constant sensation. The doctor assured me my legs would be okay, but he said I would need an operation to clean the wounds thoroughly. I had been wearing a chemical suit when we were ambushed. The suit, meant to protect the skin from chemical attack, was lined with charcoal, charcoal that had been embedded in my wounds and was a potential source of a serious infection. He was calling it surgery because they would be knocking me out to clean out the wounds. If they had to do surgery just to clean out the charcoal, I figured the threat of infection had to be serious.

"I will do my best to care for you," he said. "We must show the world our humanity."

I figured he was missing the point. You either had it, and people knew it, or you didn't. Humanity wasn't something you should have to demonstrate, but I kept my mouth shut and he finished his work. I could tell, from his touch and the way he bandaged my wounds, that he was a skilled doctor. I trusted that he was doing the best he could for me.

The first day set the pattern for most of the days in the prison. The doctor would come to check on my wounds and offer words of encouragement that my legs were healing. That first day, he must have told the guards to give me a new set of the prison pajamas. The set I had been issued the night before were ruined with my blood. The new set had faded yellow stripes and I wondered how long it would be before I could wear my own clothes again.

The soldier who acted the part of the nurse would come and give me shots of antibiotics, the same serious expression on his face. The doctor would visit the guys who were injured as well. Hernandez had been shot in the arm. Hudson had been shot twice, but he still demanded to see the doctor's credentials before he would allow him to examine him. He would also demand to see literature on any of the drugs he was given. I couldn't believe it when the doctor complied with the demands.

A guard would periodically offer me trips to the bathroom. "WC?" the guard would ask. I would shuffle down the hall, where I began to use torn strips from my brown Army T-shirt as toilet paper. I slowly shredded the shirt from the bottom up, wondering what I would do when that ran out.

As the first day wore on, I could hear cell doors opening and closing as each of the men was offered a trip to the bathroom and it wasn't long before I was assured by the sounds that all of us were in the same prison, the men scattered in cells down the hall from me.

Breakfast usually consisted of a horrible gruel, not oatmeal, not grits, but some tasteless, watery, tan-colored horror I couldn't eat no matter how hungry I was. I usually left it congealing in the bottom of my bowl, rejecting it each morning as if some alternative were possible. My bowl and spoon were my responsibility to clean each day. I would take my utensils with me as I hobbled down the hall to the WC and wash them using a primitive hose and basin that was just outside the toilet.

Lunch was usually a bowl of rice and every other day there would be chicken in it. Sometimes stewed tomatoes were sprinkled on top. One day we were given thin slices of cucumber on top of the rice, but most days we were served plain sticky white rice. Dinner came with a hard bread roll and more rice. They left us each day with a pitcher of water and a plastic cup. Each meal was accompanied by extremely sweet hot tea, tiny leaves of the brew floating at the bottom of the glass. I always drank the tea, knowing that the water had been boiled.

The march of the hours was marked by the calls to prayer that came from the mosques' loudspeakers five times a day. It felt as if the minarets were right outside the prison walls as the warbling song seeped through my small window and bounced loudly around inside my cell.

And every day, the sounds of war rattled my nerves—the bleat of AK-47 fire and explosions, sometimes far away, sometimes so close I could smell the sulfur of gunpowder in the air. They were constant reminders that a war was going on out there. Bombs often shook the prison walls and I realized there was every possibility that I could be killed by an American bomb.

The war noises scared me but I was also reassured that there were American soldiers out there. I hoped they were looking for us. I prayed we would be rescued before one of those bombs found our prison as a target.

All day long that first day, I worried that at any moment I would be further interrogated, that they had found the notebook I hid in the truck, that they had discovered that I was a liar and that I knew more than I was telling. I was on constant alert for sounds in the hallway that would indicate they were coming for me. By the end of the day I was exhausted, both from fighting the constant pain in my legs and from wrestling with worry about what would happen next.

So when darkness had fallen, and I was preparing for a restless night in my cell, footsteps heading to my door made my heart speed up. I sat up before the door opened. A middle-aged guard motioned that I should follow him. I was petrified. I struggled up from my sleep mat, wincing in pain, and followed his bulky frame down the long hall past several cell doors.

We came to a junction and I glanced to the left and noticed an open doorway that led to the outside. High stone walls topped in barbed wire surrounded an open courtyard. The brief glimpse was further evidence that we were inside an established prison. I wondered if the guys from my unit and I were the only prisoners in custody in the place. I hadn't heard anyone speaking Arabic other than the guards, but alone in my cell, it was hard to know what was going on outside.

I continued to follow the guard as he opened a door and

stepped inside a room. As before, men sat behind a table. This time there were only two of them. I stood in front of them, trying not to tremble.

"We are from the Red Crescent," one of them said.

I tried not to show how relieved I was. The Red Crescent is the Middle Eastern version of the Red Cross. These men weren't here to interrogate me, but to help if they could.

"We have come to gather information of your capture. You will be treated as a prisoner of war according to the Geneva Convention rules," the man explained further.

They gave me a small card to complete that asked for basic information like my name, my parents' names, and their address. I filled out the information wondering how my parents would react to receiving the card. They had to know by now that I had been captured.

When I finished with the card, they asked, "Is there anything you need?"

I thought about my shredded T-shirt and the disgusting squat toilet I was forced to use and it was easy to answer.

"I'd like some toilet paper," I said.

They looked at me as if I had lost my mind, complete incomprehension written on their faces. "Have you seen a doctor?" they asked, ignoring what they didn't or wouldn't understand.

"Yes," I replied.

And that was that. I was returned to my cell and listened as each of the guys was brought out and escorted down the hall for his turn. Miller wouldn't go easily. "What do you want?" he said when his door was opened. "Where are we going?"

"Shut up! Shut up!" were the angry responses he always received, but he had to lip off anyway.

Miller liked to stir up the guards and he was good at it. He really got them riled up with a Toby Keith song. He would sing it at the top of his lungs, belting out the insulting lyrics like he was slapping each of the guards individually in the face.

Oh, justice will be served and the battle will rage:
This big dog will fight when you rattle his cage.
An' you'll be sorry that you messed with the U.S. of A.
'Cos we'll put a boot in your ass, it's the American way.

Now, you have to understand that Miller cannot sing, but he would belt out that song like he had the pipes to back it up. The guards probably couldn't understand the lyrics, but they could definitely understand the sentiment behind the singing coming out of that cell. Miller would sing and the guards would immediately start shouting at him to shut up. He would just sing louder. The first time he did it, I was so afraid for him. I thought they might just take him out and shoot him. What would stop them? He was being a troublemaker and that's what happens to troublemakers, isn't it? But Miller kept singing and the guards kept telling him to shut up and nothing happened to him.

The guy had only been in the Army six months when we left on that convoy. Only six months, and he had been firing on and killing the enemy during that attack that led to our capture, fighting until his weapon malfunctioned and he was overwhelmed. He was still fighting even though he was wearing prisoner-of-war pajamas and gray plastic sandals.

When everyone had been down the hall, I lay on my mattress listening to the prison going to sleep. I knew I would have a restless night worrying about my family, wondering if I would be interrogated again, praying for rescue. Despite the worry, I somehow managed to get a few hours of sleep.

The next morning, the routine began again. The doctor came. The nurse came and gave me a shot. I made my trip to the bathroom. I didn't eat the nasty breakfast gruel. I heard the calls to prayer and felt the building shake from explosions.

On that second morning, I heard a voice I didn't recognize striking up a conversation with one of the guards. "So, are you married? Got any kids?" This stranger was talking to the guard as if it was perfectly natural to converse with them.

"Shut up! No talking," the guard responded.

Then another voice I didn't recognize with a heavy southern accent: "Hey, can I have a Coke? Coca-Cola?" he asked mockingly, as if the guard was too stupid to understand.

"Shut up! No talking," the guard responded.

Later that day, I heard Riley talk to the two new voices quietly through the cell doors while the guards were somewhere else. They were Apache pilots who had been shot down the same night our convoy had been attacked. Chief Warrant Officer Ron Young was the one who asked for a Coke as if he were ordering room service. Chief Warrant Officer Dave Williams liked to strike up conversations with the guards, winning them over with kindness. I was sorry our group had grown, that these men had been captured, but I was relieved by their attitude. They both seemed relaxed, as if they knew what to expect. I knew that as helicopter pilots, they had received mandatory training so they would know what to do if they were ever shot down and taken prisioner. Their attitude helped ease some of my tension.

Riley handed over leadership of us to Chief Williams since he was no longer the highest-ranking man, telling him about us, how many of us there were, and that there was a female in the group.

It dawned on me that my being a woman could complicate things for the guys. I remembered the scene in the movie *G.I. Jane* where Demi Moore and her classmates are going through a course to teach them about survival tactics in case they are taken prisoner. The interrogators abuse the woman to make her fellow squad members attempt to protect her, to prevent her beating. I didn't want to be a tool, and I vowed to myself I would do my best not to put any of the guys in danger.

The long hours alone in my cell started to get to me. I cried sometimes and had conversations with God. Lonely. I simply felt profoundly lonely. I thought about that last mass I had attended and the words of the chaplain, and then like an old friend, that song from the mass was in my head again. It had felt good to sing it during the mass, so I thought I'd give it a try, see if it would help. I sang it quietly at first, but the words and the singing did make me feel better, so I just belted it out.

> *Amazing grace, how sweet the sound,*
> *That saved a wretch like me . . .*
> *I once was lost but now am found,*
> *Was blind but now I see.*

I expected the guards to interrupt me at any moment. "Shut up! No singing!" I expected them to say, but they never did. So I sang. I sang all the words I could remember. It helped.

16

Body Art

I was introduced to the man I call the Irishman when I went to the bowling alley on Fort Bliss with some friends. I was immediately attracted to the six-foot-tall, burly-looking man with the reddish brown hair and green eyes. He had large tattoo sleeves on both arms, and after talking to him for a while, I realized his tongue was pierced. I thought he was cool. He was a soldier and I liked that about him, too.

He was the first man I ever fell in love with, in love so bad it made me stupid. Over and over again we broke up and got back together, broke up and somehow found ourselves right back together again. I couldn't shake my attraction to him. He wasn't intimidated by my independence and in fact he built up my confidence, always telling me I could do things if I set my mind to it. At first, he encouraged me to join the military, but he somehow cooled to the prospect the closer I got to actually doing it. I joined anyway and that was the cause of yet another of our breakups. Over all the time I knew him, I never seemed to give anyone else a chance, since I always thought we would end up together. Stupid in love.

One thing we had in common was our tattoos. I'm not sure why I got my first one, but a friend and I just decided one day to try it. I decided on a tattoo of a crouching panther that looks like it's crawling up my thigh. The process, while painful, is somehow addictive, so I had to get a few more. The Egyptian queen Nefertari is the second tattoo I have. I wanted that strong woman on my shoulder when I went through basic training. At my first duty station, I had the Egyptian symbol for eternal life, called an ankh, tattooed on the back of my left shoulder. The ankh looks like a cross with an upside-down teardrop shape at the top. The eyes of Ra, the symbol of the Egyptian sun god, are at the small of my back. The eyes are topped by a tribal symbol that looks like eyebrows. I added the black-and-white symbol for POW/MIA above the eyes of Ra along with the date of our capture. I meant it as a symbol to remember all those who died that day, including the Marines who did their best to get us out and died in the process.

My most recent tattoo is made up of the words *Magnificent Seven,* with *Magnificent* at the top and the word *Seven* slashing down and to the left forming the number 7. Across the bottom of the number, I have the initials DRJJEPS etched into the small of my back. It was something Joe came up with: Dr. J. Jeps was the name he devised that meant all of us—Dave, Ron, Joe, Jim, Edgar, Patrick, and Shana. I have the initials tattooed permanently on my skin since they will all be in my life permanently.

I was at my first duty station at Fort Carson when I decided to have my tongue pierced. The Irishman had a pierced tongue and there was something about the idea that appealed. I thought it was cool and I wanted to try it. He had often suggested that I have my nipples pierced as well, but I had resisted the idea. After having my tongue done, and after we had broken up yet another time, suddenly it didn't sound like such a bad idea. I had my nipples pierced out of pure spite.

We talked about getting married. I was twenty-nine and wanted Janelle to have a baby brother or sister. I wanted to have the Irishman's baby, but he said he wasn't ready, wouldn't be ready for ten years or more. I didn't want to wait, so we broke up again. Four months later, he married someone else, and to add insult to injury, she was a woman in my unit. That was when I had my nipples pierced. To make matters worse, when two years later he divorced, I dated him for a brief period yet again. Yes. Stupid.

I wasn't much smarter about men when it came to Janelle's father. We never had much of a relationship before she was born, let alone after. For a long time, he didn't want to be a part of her life. He ended up marrying someone in my unit and they have two kids together. I would keep him up-to-date on what was happening with Janelle, but he seemed reluctant to get too involved and even reluctant for me to have any contact with his wife. I guess he thought we wouldn't get along. She is a great person, and despite the way her husband acted, she knew that he needed to have a better relationship with his daughter. She and I talked several times, making a few tentative efforts to get to know one another. Finally, last year, Janelle and I went for a visit, and Janelle, at six years old, met her father and his family for the first time. It was awkward at first, but we all ended up getting along very well and I'm glad that Janelle will now know her father and her stepbrothers. We plan future visits and we both look forward to them.

The father of my child will always be a part my life. And somehow, the Irishman, who is married now and has a son of his own, has left a mark on my life that won't go away. He saw me for me, saw things in me I'm not sure too many others see. For the most part, people take one look and make assumptions. There are a lot of things about me one might miss on a passing inspection, like my Panamanian heritage, my career as a soldier, my piercings, my love of rock and roll and country music. The Irishman seemed to see that there was more to me than what can be seen on the surface, or at least he made me believe that he could. I'm not perfect. I've made lots of mistakes. I've certainly made mistakes when it comes to relationships, but I'm my own person, have my own likes and dislikes. Maybe someday I'll find someone who will understand all that.

17

Surgery

When the doctor came on the fourth day of my captivity, he told me he needed X-rays of my chest to prepare for my surgery. I wasn't sure why he needed a chest X-ray for surgery on my legs, but I trusted him and shuffled down the hall with him. We entered a room where he had a small portable X-ray machine set up.

I figured I'd better tell him what he would see in the X-ray. "I should tell you that I'm wearing nipple rings," I said. His eyes got large, and there was a long pause as he tried to digest my words.

"I see," he said.

"Do you want me to take them out?" I asked him.

"No," he said quickly. "That will not be necessary."

He avoided looking me in the eye as he positioned me in front of the machine. He took the films he needed, then handed me a piece of paper.

"You must write a consent letter, authorizing us to perform your surgery," he said.

I almost laughed. I had to give them permission to cut me open? Wasn't I their prisoner? But I wrote a simple note saying they had my permission to perform the operation. Once the document was signed he escorted me back to my cell. I figured Hudson would have asked for an attorney before he would have written such a thing!

"You will have the operation tomorrow," the doctor said. "Do not eat until I come for you again, for the surgery," he instructed, and he left.

I was nervous about having surgery but my legs weren't getting any better. After four days, I was still losing blood, still bleeding through the bandages, and my wounds looked raw and horrible. Pain was my constant companion. I figured anything they could do to help the wounds would be better than doing nothing.

I lay down that night, not sure if I could sleep, nervous about the surgery. A couple of hours later my cell door opened. The light from the hallway suddenly spilled into the small room, blinding me for several moments. The doctor, the nurse, and a guard were there. They stood me up and blindfolded me using a sleep mask. They didn't bother tying my hands this time. They shuffled me down the halls of the prison and I could hear them getting others out of their cells. I figured it was Hudson and Hernandez, the others who had been wounded. The doctor hadn't told me we would all be going, but I was glad not to be going alone. They took us all outside, propping me up along the way.

For a few brief moments, I was outside, the night air seeming crisp and refreshing after so much time in the confines of my cell. After a couple of seconds, I smelled cordite from all of the automatic gunfire I had been hearing and suddenly realized how close the fighting must have been. I smelled fire, stuff burning, and the general rot that comes from too many smells mixed together.

They quickly hustled us into the back of a truck and we took off into the night. We were all jounced around in the back as we careened through the streets, automatic weapons fire and the thump of small explosions going off all around us. Occasionally I heard a high scream and then a sudden heavy boom that could only mean a U.S. bomb. The Iraqis didn't have stuff like that. It was impossible to figure out where it was coming from as we turned and swerved down the streets.

It was horrible being blindfolded, not knowing where we were going, not able to see where the firing was coming from. Much of it was close. I knew the driver was going fast to avoid being a target. As nervous as I was about the surgery and about getting hit by some random bullet, it felt good to know that Americans were close. I rode in the truck silently rooting for my side to kick some righteous ass.

We finally arrived at our destination. A gust of warm night air hit me when someone opened the back of the truck. Two people grabbed me under each arm, pulled me out of the truck, and stood me up. Then someone grabbed my right arm and led me inside a building. I had a hard time keeping up with him, my legs were throbbing, and I almost stumbled and fell.

After a time, they removed the sleep mask that served as my blindfold. I was standing in a brightly lit operating room. Two unfamiliar men dressed in green surgical scrubs stood on the opposite side of an operating table, their faces far from friendly. Over their heads, strips of duct tape decorated two small windows to prevent the glass from shattering into the room. Just then, two large explosions rocked the building and made the windows rattle violently in the frames, confirming the purpose of the tape. The men cringed slightly and looked angry that I had witnessed their nervousness.

The room was clean and done up in light blue tile. The operating table, draped in green surgical cloth and surrounded by out-of-date medical equipment, looked like stuff from a 1950s science-fiction film. A nearby table full of shiny silver medical instruments was worrisome. I didn't much like the look of any of it.

A third man with a video camera leaned against the wall. *Smart,* I thought. Record the whole thing so that if anything went wrong they could say they had done all they could. The camera could have made me feel better knowing that there would be a record of what these men did to me, but it didn't. I felt helpless, nervous, and my freaking legs were killing me. I would be under anesthetic with no idea what they were going to do to me. I couldn't get a second opinion. I was at their mercy and I didn't much like it.

The doctor pointed to one of the men. "This is your anesthesiologist," he said. He pointed to the other man and said, "This is doctor to do your operation."

The videographer moved closer and wasn't shy about putting the camera right in my face. He wore surgical scrubs over his dark suit. His smoky eyes and serious expression led me to believe he had little sympathy for my plight. He obviously wasn't a friend. He moved about getting shots and everyone else in the room ignored him.

They maneuvered me onto the table.

"Have you ever had surgery before?" asked the anesthesiologist.

"No."

"Are you scared?"

I thought to myself, *Of course I'm scared! Wouldn't you be?* But what I said was, "Yes."

"Ah, first surgery and in Baghdad," he said in a deadpan joke delivery. Everyone in the room burst into laughter. It pissed me off a little that they were laughing.

Suddenly a huge explosion rocked the building, followed closely by another that rattled the windows. Everyone in the room, including me, instinctively ducked. Those were American bombs going off around us. *Yeah! Who's laughing now?!* I thought to myself. After the violence of the explosions, we all straightened up and eyed each other nervously. They were about to operate on me when my country was bombing the hell out of their capital city. I wondered if they all hated me. I wondered what I would think of them if the tables were turned.

Without further talking, they began to move with some urgency. Both doctors put their hands on my shoulders to lay me down. They simply rolled up the legs of the yellow-striped pajama suit I had been wearing and I was grateful I wouldn't be naked in front of these men. I watched as the anesthesiologist inserted an IV line into my hand and pushed a drug through.

I hoped that when this was over, my legs would feel better. I was fearful of infection. They told me the purpose of the surgery was to clean out the wounds, but I wondered what else they would do, what the real details and extent of my injuries were. I was bleeding through the bandages every day and my legs weren't getting better.

I was scared shitless and the war was feeling very close, just outside the building. I heard all that firing, those bombs going off, and knew people were dying around me. I didn't want surgery but it had to be done. Besides, it wasn't like I had many choices.

I said a little prayer, and then I lost consciousness.

18

Waking Up

My first lucid thought was to wonder what was wrong with my left leg. I tried to move it and then panicked for a second when I didn't recognize the feel of the limb. I sat up quickly to see for myself why it didn't feel natural. My foot and ankle were encased in a plaster half cast that sat heavily on a stack of folded blankets to keep it elevated. I stared at the thick wads of cotton that were poking up from the top of the cast. I'm not sure what I expected my leg to look like after the surgery, but this wasn't it. Later, I would be very grateful for that cotton.

The right leg had been operated on, too. The fresh bandages were thicker than before and covered my ankle and calf. I was still heavily medicated, so I couldn't tell if anything was really better, but I wasn't feeling any pain and that was a relief.

The doctor appeared at my bedside and pushed me back down, telling me to relax. I was in a brightly lit room. Two serious-looking guys in civilian clothes with machine pistols strapped to their chests were standing guard. I wonder if they were there to protect me from some threat since it didn't make sense to guard against my trying to make a run for it or something. It should have been obvious I wasn't going anywhere.

I looked past one of the guards and saw Hudson as they rolled him into the room. One of the guards noticed me looking and attempted to use his body to block my view.

"Is he okay?" I asked the doctor.

"Yes, of course he is okay. Why do you ask?" the doctor said.

"Because he's my friend." Just as I answered, I could hear Hudson across the way from me.

"Is she okay?" he asked.

I wasn't sure if he got an answer to his question.

We had been blindfolded when we arrived so I never saw Hernandez there in the hospital, but I knew his injuries required surgery, too, so I figured he must be somewhere nearby. I must have been in and out of consciousness waiting for whatever would happen next. It was obvious that we were in a civilian hospital. I didn't see any other patients but I saw doctors and the occasional nurse dressed in white and wearing a Muslim veil on her head. I never saw the guards warn anyone away, but the mean-looking dudes were enough of a formidable presence close by that I'm sure no one would have tried.

Finally they blindfolded me again and I was aware of my gurney rolling down the hallway and of being loaded into an ambulance. In no time we were on our way back to the prison. This time, the streets were quiet on the twenty-minute ride back. We were still going fast, or it felt like we were in my blindfold, but we weren't dodging bullets and bombs.

The sounds of war had been intense on the way to the hospital. I figured all of that violence had to mean the Iraqis probably had plenty of their own wounded to care for. Instead they were using an ambulance and their doctors to care for Hudson,

Hernandez, and me. I wondered why they would do that. I was grateful, but it also made me curious about their motives.

At the prison, they wheeled me on my gurney into my cell. I didn't recognize the place. Pushed against the wall in the tiny room was an honest-to-goodness hospital bed. I expected to see the thin mattress I had been sleeping on and hadn't thought about how difficult it would be to get up and down on it in my present state. They had stacked a pile of wool blankets at the foot of the bed to keep my leg elevated.

I looked at the care they had taken, the thought they had put into making me comfortable after the surgery, and it made me cry. They were being kind. They were being thoughtful. I was in pain and feeling alone and scared out of my wits and their small kindness moved me to tears.

I choked back the sniffles and wondered why. Why would they go to such trouble to make me comfortable? Did they expect something from me? Did they think being kind would benefit them in some way? I didn't know and it wasn't something I was likely to find out. I simply felt grateful that I wouldn't be forced to struggle with that mattress on the floor.

They got me situated on my new bed and it wasn't long before I was out again. I must have slept for hours because when I woke up, any traces of pain medication were gone. I was startled fully awake to the worst pain I had ever felt. Both legs throbbed with sharp stabbing jabs and I involuntarily groaned in agony. I lay there for only a few moments hurting, wondering how I would handle the agony, when a guard opened the door. He was a new face, very young, and someone I hadn't seen before, but he must have been instructed to listen for me because as soon as he saw that I was awake, he brought the nurse to me.

It was the same nurse who had been treating me all along,

giving me shots of antibiotics and assisting the doctor on his visits. He didn't speak a word of English and he and I had never been very good at communicating with each other, but this time he didn't need much translation to know what I needed. They had left an intravenous catheter in my hand after the surgery. He gave me pain medications through the catheter, and whatever it was brought relief very quickly. I was knocked out for hours. By the time I woke again, the sun was shining through my cell window.

I lay there much of the day, dozing in and out of sleep. I wished for something to read or music to listen to, something to occupy my mind other than its wild bounces from worry to fear to longing thoughts of home. I wondered where Lynch was. The doctor had told me she was alive and I wondered why she wasn't with us. As mangled as her truck was, I figured she must have been injured. If that were the case, maybe she had been in the same hospital where I had my surgery. It was all speculation, but I had plenty of time on my hands and plenty of theories to roll around in my head.

I prayed a lot. My conversations with God usually centered on my parents, my daughter, and my sisters. I prayed they wouldn't worry too much. I knew Janelle would be fine and well cared for, but I prayed she would stay ignorant of my predicament and somehow be protected from the worry.

I heard the thump of explosions, the bleat of automatic weapons fire, and sometimes helicopters flying overhead. The war was right outside and I lay in that hospital bed and listened to it. I cringed at the explosions that shook the walls of the building and wondered if a prison would be a target for American bombs. The prayer I most often repeated was that if I was going to go, if I was going to die, if some stray bomb was destined to find our building or if the Iraqis were to decide they were done with us, I wanted it to be quick.

"Lord, just let me go out quick," I prayed. No lingering. No torture, just lights-out. And I prayed that if I was going to die, my body would be found. I didn't want my parents or my daughter to be left without evidence of my death. I didn't want them to have to wonder what happened to me, so I prayed they would have a body to bury if it came to that.

When the worry got to be too much and I needed solace, I sang my song, "Amazing Grace," and none of the guards told me to shut up.

Sometime later, a distinguished-looking man in uniform came to visit me. He must have been an important guy because the guards showed him a lot of deference, which he took as if it were his due. His English was impeccable. He explained that he was some kind of chief of surgery for the military; I didn't get the exact title, but it was obvious that he was conducting an inspection to ensure we were getting proper medical care. The guards were bowing and scraping and going out of their way to make sure he was happy with the care we received.

"Are you okay?" he asked me.

"Yes, I'm doing fine," I said.

He nodded as if everything met with his approval. "You will be fine," he said. "They will take good care of you."

He inspected my tiny cell. I couldn't get myself to the bathroom anymore, so the guards had provided me with a bucket. It was a source of humiliation for me, that bucket. There was no way I could get down the hall, so I didn't have much choice. The inspector eyed the bucket and instructed the guards to ensure it was kept underneath the bed and out of sight. I didn't like them discussing it. Hiding it as much as possible was the only solution to an otherwise uncomfortable subject.

The inspector surgeon was joined, a bit later, by another important guy. It was getting kind of crowded in my little room. The second guy was a pudgy man with thick reddish hair and a big bushy mustache. He peered at me kindly and asked, "Do you need anything?"

By this time, I hadn't had a shower in a week, and I had been wearing the same unwashed sports bra and panties since the day we left Camp Virginia. If I could have one wish, I knew exactly what I would wish for.

"I'd like a clean pair of underclothes," I said.

He paused for a long moment, as if unsure of what he heard, and then he nodded slowly. I'm sure the surgeon with the impeccable English helped with the translation if any was needed.

Like my request for toilet paper, I figured they were only asking because it was what they were expected to do. I was never given any toilet paper and I figured this much more complicated request would go equally ignored. Still, I couldn't help but think about how nice it would be to have another clean white sports bra and a fresh pair of cotton underwear. What I got the next day wasn't that. One of the guards came in and handed me a neatly folded stack, and one could not help but immediately notice the color.

He handed me a matching set of bloodred underclothes—a red bra and red panties—along with a pink T-shirt. I looked at that lingerie—because with that color and fabric you couldn't call them simply underwear, this was something much more lingerie-ish than underwear-ish—with my mouth hanging open and wondered what these guys were thinking. Maybe it was some kind of a cultural misunderstanding on my part, but where I come from, a gift of red lingerie meant things were expected to get intimate right quick. I didn't know whether to be thankful or frightened.

I sat in shock for several seconds, then realized the guard was still standing there. I could see from his expression that he hadn't meant to offend but wanted to know if the delivery had been met with approval. I said the only thing I could come up with.

"Thank you."

"Okay," he said.

He finally left and I changed my underclothes and felt some immediate relief. I tried not to speculate about what, if anything, the red color meant.

Later that day, Young, Williams, Riley, and Miller were taken out of their cells and out of the prison. I listened as their doors were opened and I could hear them being herded into the hallway and taken out. I even heard them loaded into a vehicle and I heard the vehicle drive away.

I was petrified for them. They had all been lippy, belligerent, and demanding with the guards and the guards had shown little patience with them. At every opportunity, they had shown defiance. Miller seemed to take the brunt of the guards' anger. He would sing his song, "The Angry American," and the guards would go into a frenzy of screaming at him. Sometimes I could hear the guards go into his cell in an attempt to make him shut up. I thought they might have beaten him. The singing would stop, but if they had laid hands on him or struck him in any way, Miller took it without a sound, a fact that wouldn't surprise me from the young soldier.

One day, after we had been in the prison for several days, they suddenly decided to take Miller's wedding ring away. The guards entered his cell and I could hear them demanding that he hand the ring over. Miller, true to form, refused. The ruckus that followed went on for a long time. I know they struck him several times. The noise sounded horrible.

"Stop!" I shouted at them. "Leave him alone!" But the guards ignored me. A few seconds later I appealed to Miller. "Give it to them, Miller. Just give it to them!" I didn't want him to be beaten anymore. I knew his wife would rather he hand over the symbol of their marriage than go through a severe beating. But the man was stubborn. He fought hard to keep that ring, but eventually they took it from him. I wondered what the loss meant to him.

Not long after the guards left his cell, Miller launched into the Toby Keith song again, singing about justice and rage and putting a boot in someone's ass. The guy was brave. Maybe a little crazy, but brave.

Now they were all being herded out and taken somewhere. I wanted to believe the four men were selected to go because they weren't recovering from surgery. Part of me worried that I wouldn't see or hear from them again. I was so sure they were going to be shot or worse. I wanted to ask Hudson and Hernandez what they thought, but I couldn't talk to them through the walls.

I felt lonely in my cell that night. I sat up waiting as the minutes ticked by. I waited and worried and prayed I would see them all again. Every second crept by.

Finally, after several hours, the men came back. They were led back down the hall and let back into their cells. I listened as each cell door closed, counting them in my head to be sure each man was accounted for. I wondered what had happened, where they had been taken, but at that point, all I cared about was that they were back and we were all together again.

19

Woman Stuff

I stood on the line at the DFAC (dining facility) at Fort Carson, Colorado, and felt their eyes on me. I can't remember what I was serving that day, grits or pancakes or creamed beef on toast. I stood on the other side of the breakfast buffet line, serving the food we had prepared that morning, pretending I didn't notice the stares. It was a large DFAC and the line snaked out toward the door and I knew I would be standing there for a couple of hours, hearing the mumbling and feeling the stares.

"They got a woman in here now?" I heard one soldier say. "Where did she come from?"

The DFAC where I normally worked was closed while everyone who usually ate there was out in the field on an exercise. I was sent to work temporarily in a different kitchen for a unit made up exclusively of men. They were acting like they'd never seen a woman before, so they were staring and making quiet comments but it wasn't a big deal. I knew the novelty would wear off quickly, and soon I would be just another soldier asking them if they wanted bacon or sausage. At the time, on my first day, I was the only woman in the room, the only one in the kitchen. Weeks later, a few more women would be assigned to the unit, and having a woman around would be commonplace.

We're still outnumbered by a long shot, but as far as I'm concerned, being a woman in the Army is no big deal anymore. You grow accustomed to being the only woman in the room, to being around men all the time, to having only a few females available to hang out with. It takes a while for the men to get comfortable with your presence. They might test you to see the limits of your tolerance for their brash talk, to see if you'll ask them to lift the heavy stuff, if you'll expect special treatment because you're a woman. Once all that is sorted, you become just another member of the team. There are some advantages, too. The fewer the women, the fewer people you might have to share a tent with, the better the chances you can have a room to yourself, and the shorter the lines for a bathroom or shower.

The challenges that come with being a woman in the Army aren't about being outnumbered. The challenges are about simply being a woman. Challenges like what to do if you have to go to the bathroom when you're on a long convoy and what to do with your hair.

Part of my preparation for the long deployment away from home was to make a plan for how I would manage my hair. I was going to war. It was entirely possible that I might find myself in a place where there wouldn't be anyone around who could help me with it. There are plenty of people in the world who are ignorant about what it takes to manage black hair. It's not a matter of running a comb through it or tossing it into a cute little ponytail. I required a plan. I brought a curl relaxer with me, thinking that once we got settled, I could relax it and that would make the management of it easier, but until then, I had to get it braided.

Before I left Fort Bliss, I asked a neighbor lady who had done it before to add some extensions to my hair and to braid it into tight cornrows. I figured I could wear it like that for a month, and by that time, I hoped I would find someone who had the skills to braid and could help me maintain it.

Mrs. Lawson did a great job, making the braids tight enough that I knew I wouldn't have to worry about them. She chatted with me as she pulled and tucked and created a nice uniform pattern of braids around my head.

"I wish you didn't have to go over there," she said, shaking her head and tsking her disapproval under her breath.

"I'll be okay," I told her. "You don't have to worry about me."

She made the braids especially tight, knowing they would have to last for a while. It took her a much longer time than usual, and when I tried to pay her for the service, she refused to accept my money.

"Oh no, no, no," she said to me. "You just make sure you come back safe."

I didn't realize I would be wearing those same braids for so many weeks, but the job she did solved my hair problems for quite some time. There wasn't anything Mrs. Lawson could do, though, to solve my bathroom problems.

As a last resort, a man can take a piss in a bottle if he has to on a long convoy. Not only did I not have that easy relief, the idea of dropping my drawers and leaving my ass exposed to the wide-open desert was not appealing. I hated the vulnerability of it, the idea that we could be going into a war zone where I would have to find a shrub for shelter and crouch with my M16 strapped across my back in order to take a leak.

While I was at Fort Carson in a unit that was all cavalry soldiers, I heard about a device we could order through the supply system that allowed women to pee standing up. It was a triangular paper trough that caught the urine in a sort of a funnel and directed it away from your body so you could actually pee standing up. I thought it was ingenious. We even had a national stock number for the thing, a thirteen-digit number used to order military supplies. It was all the information we needed to order the devices, so I was surprised when I ran into resistance. I gave all of the information to the supply folks at Fort Bliss hoping we could order them before we left, but they weren't convinced.

"Oh, you won't need this," they said. "You can just go outside like you guys always have. Why would you want to pee standing up?"

I tried to convince them that it was a simple thing that would make convoys and field conditions easier for us women to handle, but the request was never taken seriously or it simply didn't take priority over other things needed for the trip. It was a high priority for us, so a bunch of the women in the unit ordered a supply of the disposable devices through a civilian supplier and they arrived just four days before we left for Kuwait.

It took a while for me to figure out how to use the paper trough without peeing down my pant leg, but eventually I got the hang of it. As it turned out, our separated segment of the convoy had to stop so many times to help trucks that had broken down that I had plenty of opportunity to work on my skills. There was never any shelter in the form of trees or shrubs to hide behind and I didn't want to walk too far away from the convoy and the feeling of safety its numbers provided. When the stops were brief, I stood behind the truck to relieve myself. It was strange, but standing to pee was a huge relief and far better than dropping my pants out there in the middle of nowhere. When standing behind the truck wasn't necessary, I sometimes crawled under the truck to go to the bathroom the old-fashioned way.

"Edgar, I gotta go," I would tell Hernandez. He would stay in the truck, keeping an eye out and waiting for the signal to leave.

"Johnson, come on!" he would yell.

"I'm coming," I'd say, and scramble to get my pants pulled up and get back into the truck.

Aside from taking a leak, I had to consider the possibility that I might get my period at some inopportune time during the deployment. I saw my ob-gyn before we left and asked him about a method I had heard about from other soldiers. They said you could skip the week of sugar pills in the birth-control pill pack. If I never took the week of sugar pills, it would be possible to avoid having my period for months at a time.

"Go ahead and do it," he said. "It's not going to do your body any harm, and since you're going to be deployed and you don't know what the conditions will be like, you won't have to worry about infections or not having the supplies you need."

I figured I could follow that advice until we were at least in a stable place where it would be easier to deal with the problems and logistics of a menstrual cycle. I guess my body didn't adjust to the idea too well because I had my period for eleven days while we were in Kuwait. I kept up with the program, though, because I sure didn't want to have to deal with my period while we were in the middle of movement.

As our segment of the convoy fell farther and farther behind the main body, the truck Hernandez and I were in was one of the last in the movement. If a truck broke down or got stuck, we couldn't just go past them. There was no one coming after us, no more help on the way. For much of the trip, the convoy was traveling off-road, tooling through the open desert with nothing under us but Iraqi sand. The trucks in our group were heavy vehicles carrying things like fuel, tires, all kinds of equipment, and the massive trucks would sink to the axles and had to be towed or dug out to get moving again. The guys driving wreckers, the huge trucks that had the nasty job of pulling vehicles out of the sand, were constantly busy. Two soldiers driving one of the wreckers, Sergeant George Buggs and PFC Edward Anguiano, had fallen behind the main convoy trying to free a fuel tanker. They had the huge tanker truck hooked up on their winch and the unwieldy combination of wrecker and tanker had slowed them down. Dowdy told them to fall in with our group. The more trucks got stuck and broke down, the more we fell behind the main body of the convoy.

First Sergeant Dowdy, with Pie as his driver, was in charge of our group of stragglers. He herded us along, making sure we got back on the road as soon as we could. He would move from truck to truck, reminding us to eat something from our MREs, to drink water, and to grab some sleep when we could. I had taken a dislike to Dowdy when he first joined the unit. His strictness and hard exterior had grated at first meeting, but in the desert on that convoy, I appreciated the way he kept us together. When our group was separated from the main force, his sure leadership was sorely needed and I was grateful to have him with us.

There is something awesome about the open desert. We spent so many hours driving through it, rarely seeing anyone, blinded by the endless stretches of every shade of brown. Because we weren't following roads, it felt as if we had picked a random direction since there was very little in the way of landmarks to judge direction or distance by. It was sometimes difficult to separate the ground from the horizon. The light tan of the sand seems to go on forever, and when you do see people, they appear as if from out of nowhere.

Dowdy stopped for one group of nomads, their tent somewhere far off in the distance. A man with a small girl and two teenage boys was suddenly there along the side of our route watching us drive by. Dowdy stopped our column and approached them with a box of water. I got out of my truck and watched as he communicated with them briefly, making friends with the small gift. I took a picture of the family group with my disposable camera. They smiled a little but seemed more nervous than grateful for the gift.

"If anyone asks," he said to me, "tell them the water fell off the back of the truck."

We loaded back up and, hours later, eventually linked up with our commander, Captain King, and the vehicles that were with him. He had sat there waiting for us at the second checkpoint for hours. The checkpoint was a rather large supply outpost with fuel points, tents for sleeping, and a mess-tent area. The main body of the convoy had been there and had been able to refuel, to catch a few hours of sleep, and to even catch a meal. They had all already left long before our arrival. By the time we linked up with King, we were almost twelve hours behind the main body.

When we had first started out from Camp Virginia, the long line of trucks had been a comfort. A six-hundred-vehicle convoy is a grand sight. I hadn't ever seen anything like it. None of us had. That endless line of headlights, the massive vehicles, the surge of people and equipment moving into Iraq made me feel a part of something formidable and there was comfort in that. There was, after all, safety in those numbers. Now we were much reduced. We had eighteen vehicles trailing behind with us and two of those were being towed. In all, including the two soldiers, Buggs and Anguiano, who we had picked up on the trip, there were only thirty-three of us.

By the time we linked up with Captain King and after a quick refueling, we had no choice but to immediately set out again. While the tents looked appealing, there was no time for sleep or a leisurely meal.

I was nervous. We were still traveling off-road. Instead of the massive presence of the giant convoy, we were now a tiny speck in the middle of a vast desert. It appeared as if we had come from nowhere and were headed into nothing.

Good God, where are we? I thought. *And where the hell is everyone else?*

Our travel was punctuated by frequent stops, to help disabled vehicles, to rest, to eat, to relieve ourselves. My thinking became dull with lack of sleep, my eyes irritated by the sand kicked up in great clouds by the vehicles in front of us. My uniform, my skin, and my weapon became covered in the soft brown of the desert. Hernandez was silent, staring straight ahead, pushing through the exhaustion to drive. Just drive. The vibration and rumble of the truck sank into my bones. Stopping felt as if someone had pushed a mute button, the sudden silence and stillness a shock to my system. There were no other vehicles, no bird or insect sounds, just us and the desert silence.

Eventually we came upon a group of Marines. Their armored vehicles and trucks were lined up on the desert route. We drove past them and I watched them through my window. We were passing Marines. That didn't make sense to me. Marines were usually ahead of Army. Marines were the guys they sent into combat zones, the badasses who swooped in to save the day. Why were we passing them?

My instincts told me something wasn't right. We didn't have a radio. Hernandez and I didn't have a map and our only option was to follow where everyone else was going. The commander, Captain King, had the GPS and knew which way we were supposed to go. So we passed the Marines. There are times when being right isn't a good thing.

20

Tumbling Down

My mother, my sisters, and I were in a huge shopping mall. We went from store to store, our arms growing heavy with our purchases. We tried on clothes and shoes and bags to match and strolled lazily through the brightly lit mall, talking, enjoying each other's company. When we finally grew tired of shopping, we left the mall but couldn't remember where we had parked the car. We wandered through the rows and rows of cars, the parking lot growing ever larger, our memories of where we had put the car growing ever fainter and our mood growing ever more frustrated and frantic.

I woke up with a jolt. My eyes popped open and the walls were still reverberating from the bomb that had just gone off somewhere in the neighborhood. The ripple effect of the explosion was still thrumming through the walls of my cell. I lay there, staring up at the ceiling, waiting for my heart rate to slow, fighting back tears of frustration. The realization that I was still in that tiny, dark cell was like a pitcher of freezing water in the face.

The familiar routine began again. The gruel I couldn't eat,

the hours of boredom, someone coming to empty my bucket and exchanging it for a new, clean one. The new guard, the young one who had arrived around the time of my surgery, had taken a liking to me and flirted whenever he got the chance. He had a smoky complexion, a thin mustache, and wore civilian clothes, jeans and loosely fitting shirts. His signature was a Palestinian red-and-white-checked scarf wrapped loosely around his neck. He watched me all the time and went out of his way to tell me he wasn't married. Several times he even tried to hold my hand. I would snatch my hand away, appalled by his audacity. I was his prisoner. I didn't want him to get any ideas and worried that he might let himself into my cell sometime when no one else was around to stop him.

It always made me nervous when my door was opened and it was him, the flirt, standing there waiting to take me to the WC. He made it obvious that he knew I had little control over the situation. Once, he stroked my cheek and ran his hand down the back of my neck as if in a caress. I pulled away from him, but it didn't seem to deter him.

On one trip, he took me to the WC and attempted to hold my hand as I shuffled along, but just as he reached for me, another guard came around the corner and he quickly moved his hand away.

AHA! I thought. *You'd get in trouble if anyone caught you doing that stuff.*

After that, I knew I could simply scream and the flirt would be in hot water for taking advantage of the situation. It eased my fears but it didn't stop him from flirting.

For some unknown reason, my care was transferred to a new doctor. Gone was the distinguished-looking man with the kind eyes and the smooth English. He introduced a new doctor who was a little pudgier, had far less hair on his head, and was clean shaven. The new doctor's English was also excellent and he had a love of basketball. He was a big fan of one of the Los Angeles teams and talked about the Clippers or the Lakers, I can't remember which. He told me he worked for the Red Crescent.

"I don't know why this war," he said to me.

"I don't know either," I said. I expected him to want to discuss it further but he shrugged as if in acknowledgment of the powerlessness either of us had to affect such things.

One day, the man who ran the prison came in to check on my recovery. He had a big bushy mustache, and from the way he walked in and the way the guards deferred to him, it was pretty obvious he was the man in charge. He told me I would be fine and looked over my cell as if he approved of everything.

"I have seen your mother on television," he said.

"*My* mother?"

"Yes, of course. She looked just like you. She was on CNN," he said.

I didn't know what to say or think. My mother was on television?

"She said she no like Bush," he said.

"My mother said that?"

"Yes. She looked just like you."

It was hard to believe that my mother would go on television and talk about the president! Then I thought about why she would be on television in the first place. The media were probably swarming all over my parents, asking them for comments about my imprisonment. I knew they would be worried out of their minds, and then to have the press swoop down on them—it all made me feel frustrated that there was nothing I could do. My mom would have to be extremely stressed to say anything bad about President Bush on television.

I thought about all the pressure they must be under, all of the worry and pain they must be feeling, and it made me cry. The tears started flowing, and once they started, I couldn't stop them. I tried to hide my tears from the warden but it was no use. I think he was surprised by my reaction. Hell, I was surprised by my reaction. Thankfully he didn't hang around to watch. I buried my face in my hands and he left, closing the cell door behind him.

I cried for my family and my daughter. I cried for all of their worry. Imagining my mother on TV, the worry she must be feeling, hit home. The fear I was feeling, not knowing what would happen next—they were feeling it, too. I thought about how I would have felt if it had been Nikki or Erica in my place and I ached at the stress they must be under.

Still it was hard to imagine my mother denouncing President Bush on camera to the whole wide world. I found out later that it had been my grandmother telling the reporter exactly what she thought about the situation.

"Bush needs to stop this war and bring my granddaughter home!" she had said. Eighty years old at the time, my grandmother had never been afraid to speak her mind.

Eight days into my captivity, more than eleven days since I had had a shower, I was finally given a basin of hot water, soap, and a rag. Guards led me down to the WC, where I could stand in the tiled area and give myself a good washing. The doctor had given me some plastic bags to wrap my bandaged legs in to protect them and I used the hot water and the sliver of strong-smelling soap to finally wash the grime of the desert and the hospital and the prison away. In the real world, I would have turned my nose up at the skin-drying soap and a washcloth made from the rags of some throwaway clothing. In my prison reality, I used what they gave me and it was glorious. Primitive, but glorious.

When I got back to my cell, two of the guards had a little discussion at my cell door, their heads together, hands gesturing, looking at me, going back and forth in some kind of discussion. Finally one of them blurted out in his broken English, "You no wash your hair. Why you no wash your hair?"

I guess they had expected me to take my braids out and give my hair a good wash. Maybe they imagined I would just comb it out and that would be that. Obviously they didn't understand.

"It's not real," I said. And I pulled at one of the braids until the synthetic hair came out in my hand. Well, that got the guards all excited. They must have thought I was going crazy. Pulling your own hair out was a sure sign something wasn't right in your head, and from the looks on their faces, that's what these guys were thinking, but I laughed and tried to demonstrate that I was in fact sane. "It's not real," I tried to explain, but they didn't understand. They eyed me suspiciously, discussed it some more between themselves, then one of them left and came back with the doctor.

The doctor looked alarmed when he first came into my cell. I'm sure he was expecting to see some half-sane person going berserk. I explained my side of the story and he nodded in under-standing, staring at my hair.

"I see," he said.

I wasn't sure if he did, but he was at least able to explain that I wasn't ready for a straitjacket. The guards were right about one thing. My hair needed attention in a bad way. The braids were coming loose and the extensions were pulling out. I knew I looked a mess, and while that may seem like a trivial thing to think about while one is a prisoner of war, it had a lot to do with how I felt about things. My hair, my everything, was out of my control. I had had a bath, which went a long way toward helping me feel bet-ter, but there wasn't much else to feel cheery about. My face and arms were still covered in mosquito bites. I had been trying not to scratch, but every morning I awoke to more of them and the irritation was hard to ignore. My prisoner pajamas were dirtier by the day, I had little hope that I'd get a clean pair anytime soon, and I would have given anything for a roll of toilet paper.

Later that night, as I began to settle down to sleep, a huge explosion rocked the building, this one much closer than any we had experienced. It felt as if the bomb had fallen right next door. And this wasn't just a grenade or an RPG; this was a bomb that had been dropped from the air, dropped by American forces. There was a deafening whine, followed by a massive crunch. The ground literally leaped up beneath me and the building rocked for a long time with the reverberations. The sound echoed through my cell for several seconds and rang in my ears for a lot longer. Dust and chips of the building rained down on me. I had never heard or felt anything like it and knew in my bones that my fellow prisoners and I had come very close to being bombed into oblivion by our own forces.

As things quieted down, I realized that the guards were running away! I couldn't believe it. I could hear them shouting to each other, excited bursts of language and shuffling, then feet running down the halls, and in an instant, every one of them was gone, leaving all of us in our cells.

We knew we'd been left on our own, and we began to shout at each other through our doors.

"Is everyone okay? I need an answer," Williams shouted.

We reported to him, one by one. "I'm okay," I said when it was my turn. We were looking at the damage the explosion had caused and realized that the prison had almost fallen down around us.

"I can get out," I heard Young shout. He described the damage, saying the wall had separated from his cell door and his arms were long enough that he could reach through and unlock his own door.

"That's not a good idea, man," Williams shouted at him. "We don't know where we are, and the guards can't be far away."

I could hear the frustration in Young's voice. Freedom was literally within his reach, but he closed his door and paced around inside his cell, and we all waited for what would happen next.

It was some time before the guards began to wander back, and by the time they showed up, we were all banging on our doors because we had to go to the bathroom. We had just been frightened half to death. The expression "scare the shit out of you" has some truth to it.

As they usually did, the guards took me down the hall first. I took the opportunity to survey the blast damage with my own eyes. Young's door was indeed separated from the wall. I could see inside his cell as I passed by. The ceiling of the building appeared as if it had been lifted up and set back down in a crooked way. There was dust and debris in the hallway. The building looked as if it were held together by a wish. If we had another close call like that, the whole place would come tumbling down.

The guard had been silent on my trip to the WC. Not so when the men began their trips down the hall. The guards angrily talked to them, blaming them for the damage. "This is *you*. This was you who did this thing. This is all because of you," one of the guards said.

"Yeah, whatever!" Williams said. I could hear a bit of pride in his voice. "But you can't keep us here anymore. This whole building is going to fall down. You're going to move us, right?"

"No. This is a strong building," the guard said.

"Bullshit!" Williams said.

Oh my God, he's going to be killed, I thought. Every time one of the men gave the guards a hard time, and that was often, I thought they were going to be killed, but this situation was especially volatile. All of us had had a close call with an American bomb and the guards weren't feeling too friendly toward their American prisoners. They were angry about the attack and they were probably feeling a little ashamed for having run away as soon as the dust started to fly.

And we didn't know what havoc that bomb had wrought outside. What had been the target? Had people been killed? The guards had all run and maybe they went to see what the damage was, damage that would make them angry at their attackers.

I imagined what that huge explosion must have looked like and the damage it must have caused. During the First Gulf War, like everyone else, I had been fascinated watching CNN and the huge clouds of fire and smoke that billowed over Baghdad while we bombed the city. I imagined something like that had just happened, the geysers of flame and glowing sparks that flew in great fiery arches. The smell of it, or maybe it was just the near destruction of the building we were in, wafted through my cell window.

The explosion left me shaken. I sat in my cell, trembling at the close call. A few yards nearer in our direction and I was sure I would have been buried under rubble. I prayed to quiet my trembles, but my mood was very dark. We had come close, very close, to being killed.

The guards were still worked up and talking excitedly to each other. One of them turned on a radio and Anastacia came on! They must have found an AFN (American Forces Network) radio station, the broadcast network that supplies news and entertainment for the American military. I listened to that song and the fact that it was an American song, an American artist singing at that time, I figured, had to be a good sign.

Photo by Claude Johnson

I was about four years old in this picture and still living in Panama.
My father and I wouldn't join my mother and sisters
in America until I was five. I look so serious here.
I wonder what I was thinking.

Photo by Dave Williams

LEFT: My sister Nikki was commissioned a lieutenant in a ceremony after graduating from the New Mexico Military Institute (NMMI). I was very proud of her that day. I hadn't made the decision to join the Army at the time, but we would eventually end up stationed together at Fort Carson, Colorado.

RIGHT: Colonel Joan Marks and me in Kuwait. She was one of many nurses who cared for me and also helped me through the difficulty of removing my nipple rings. I was still getting accustomed to the idea of being free.

Surrounded by the great people who helped care for me on the flight from Kuwait to Landstuhl, Germany. These are some of the unsung heroes who care for our wounded warriors returning from Iraq.

Chip was our tour guide while Janelle and I enjoyed Disneyland. We spent a day at the Magic Kingdom when we traveled to Los Angeles for my appearance on the *The Tonight Show* with Jay Leno.

I am surrounded by my mom's side of the family during an annual Panamanian Fourth of July celebration in New York City.

FAR LEFT: My cousin Andre became a drill instructor eight months after returning from a tour of duty in Iraq. He and his family were at first turned away when they came to visit me at the hospital in Landstuhl, Germany. Finally seeing him and his family was a great boost to my spirits during my recovery.

ABOVE: My father deployed to the first Gulf War as a nuclear, biological, and chemical specialist. We worried about him every day. He hated the idea that his daughters had to deploy to fight the same enemy a decade later.

BELOW: I'm all smiles when I pose for this picture with classmates after graduating from AIT (Advanced Individual Training), where I learned my MOS (Military Occupational Specialty) of 92G, Food Service Specialist.

Photo by Shoshana Johnson

My sisters and I knew how to have a good time. I'm the one on the horse wearing the hat. Erika is in the middle and Nikki rides the smaller horse. We're in a California shop not long after our family is reunited in the United States.

Photo by Claude Johnson

Photo by Eunice Johnson

Photo by Claude Johnson

ABOVE: I was three years old and hiding in my favorite tree near our home in Panama. When I revisited Panama after my release in 2003, I went back to find our old house and looked for the tree, but it was gone.

LEFT: My mom Eunice and I after I graduated from basic training. I would leave for school to be trained as an Army cook shortly after.

My aunt Sonya had this sign made and hung it on her house where it stayed the whole time I was in captivity. They didn't want anyone to forget that I was still out there.

I am ready to go and get it over with during our deployment ceremony at Fort Bliss. I wonder if I would have had such a big smile on my face if I had known what was in store for me.

Dave Williams and I pose for a picture on our first trip out in the real world after our rescue. We were treated to a meal in a restaurant located in a castle in Germany where I finally got to enjoy the steak, baked potato, and ice-cold beer I had fantasized about while in captivity.

Dr. Steven Saslow treated my injuries while I was in the hospital in Kuwait. The surgery he performed was the only one I would need to undergo along with many months of physical therapy.

LEFT: My aunt Maggie was a nurse in the Air Force and used her skills to care for me when I returned home. I still feel guilty about how horrible I was to her at times. She was the first person to diagnose that I was suffering from PTSD. RIGHT: My daughter Janelle is three years old in this picture. Despite everything, I wouldn't discourage her from becoming a soldier if that is what she wants to do.

ABOVE: My best friend Theresa Rowland came to my deployment ceremony in the gym at Fort Bliss. She's smiling here but she surprised me with tears that day. She was worried about me. I asked Lori Piestewa to take the picture of us with my camera.

LEFT: This is one of the first pictures my family took when we were all reunited in America. Erika is sitting on my dad Claude's lap, with Nikki in front of me and my mother, Eunice, standing behind. I was six years old at the time.

I am overcome with relief and bawling my eyes out in the arms of one of the Marines who rescued me. Jim Riley looks on from behind while a squad of Marines stands vigilant guard. Dave Williams and Ron Young watch from under the shelter of the track vehicle.

Minutes after our release, the Marines took out their cameras and took pictures to commemorate their successful mission. I'm grateful for this picture of me with all of the men who helped me get through the long ordeal. PFC Patrick Miller, SPC Joseph Hudson, Sergeant Jim Riley, SPC Edgar Hernandez and me, CW2 Ron Young, and CW4 Dave Williams are in front. Ron and Patrick are holding up a T-shirt that depicts the motto of the Marine Corps unit that rescued us.

Anastacia was belting out her latest hit about being stronger then before and laying it on the line. It was one of those songs that made you feel like you had to dance when you listened to it, a happy, triumphant song, and the hard-hitting music put hope in my heart. The music was so foreign to the stark and serious prison walls around me that I somehow took it to mean that we wouldn't be there long, that in the end we would be safe. In fact, the last line of the chorus was something about saying good-bye!

Yes, it was time to say good-bye to that cell, that place. I told myself I just had to hold on. Just hold on and I would get out of there, I would make it out of there alive.

21

An Nasiriyah

Anyone in the desert that night would have heard us coming long before they saw us. The rumble of our heavy trucks must have traveled for miles across the desert with few natural barriers to break up the sounds. In accordance with standard convoy operations, our headlights were on their dimmest settings and barely illuminated the ground before we drove over it. I could see the truck directly in front of us, but that was about it. We traveled off-road, hopefully following the main body of the convoy, only I couldn't see any sign of the hundreds of vehicles that had traveled the route before us. I couldn't see much of anything in the inky darkness.

We were diesel mechanics, and cooks and supply specialists. We had weapons and training and were soldiers, but combat support personnel like us are usually sent out with at least a squad of infantry or armor personnel to provide protection. Now that we were down to just eighteen vehicles in our little group, I felt vulnerable. I wondered if anyone knew how far behind the larger convoy we were. I wondered if we had been forgotten.

Dawn was still a few hours away when we crossed from the open desert onto a hard-topped road. Our tires made an entirely different but more familiar sound as we drove over real road and passed the unit of Marines. Our dim headlights flashed on them as we slowly made our way by. The Marines seemed relaxed, some grabbing sleep in their vehicles, others standing around talking, as they waited to be launched on whatever mission they were preparing for. I didn't want to pass them. I wanted to stay with them. These were Marines, the hard-core guys who knew what to do when the bullets started flying. We would be safe with them, I thought, but we were passing them by.

We learned later that it was at this point that we made our first wrong turn. We should have headed left onto Highway One, or Route Jackson, as it was called in the operations orders. Route Jackson would have taken us far to the west, skirting the city of An Nasiriyah. We apparently didn't know about taking Route Jackson, but even that mistake could have been corrected.

When we arrived on the hard-topped road, we should have run into a TCP (traffic control point), people who would have directed us exactly where to go. In convoy operations as large as ours had been, when six hundred vehicles are setting out on a trip as long as this one, the TCPs are set up at crucial junctions to make sure stragglers don't make stupid mistakes. But we were half a day behind the main body of the convoy, and for some reason—maybe our SINGARS radios were broken yet again—we had lost radio contact with our higher headquarters, the Third Forward Support Battalion.

It angers me now to think about that TCP leaving us out there. If they knew we were still out there, they shouldn't have left, no matter how far behind we were. Even if they couldn't reach us by radio, they shouldn't have left. Someone should have stayed to make sure we were headed in the right direction or someone should have come back to find out what was taking us so long. In any case, they should have known we were still out there and sent someone to see what was going on. We were eighteen vehicles and thirty-three people someone should have wondered about. If we were lost, and evidently at that point we were, then someone should have been accountable for us and come looking. We were a fraction of the larger convoy, but the Third FSB, our higher headquarters, should have wondered where in the heck we were. Evidently no one wondered.

Captain King's vehicle was the only one equipped with a plugger, the Army's version of a GPS. He also had a map with Route Blue clearly but mistakenly marked as the route we should take. For the most part, we were supposed to follow Route Blue, but the short jog around An Nasiriyah, the short period of the trip when we were to switch our route to Jackson, wasn't marked on his map. The Marines we passed were on some other mission and weren't any more aware of where we were supposed to go than we were.

A brief radio call to our higher headquarters would have straightened everything out, only our SINGARS radios, the radios we had attempted to repair over and over again at Camp Virginia, didn't work. We could have told them where we were. If they had forgotten about us, we could have reminded them that we still existed. But since we didn't have radio contact, we were left to our own devices and apparently we were so lost that we had no idea just how lost we were.

We stopped near one of the Marine vehicles and King confirmed the direction of Route Blue with them. The Marines, not knowing Blue was not our assigned route, confirmed only what they were asked.

And down the road we went. It had been over forty-two hours since we had left Camp Virginia at that point. We had had one prolonged stop where we were able to bed down for a time and try to get some sleep, but other than that, it had been straight driving, frequent stops, hours of trying to get trucks out of soft sand, and the maddeningly constant rumble of the heavy beast we were driving. Keeping my eyes open was a Herculean task. My neck was sore from the struggle to keep my head erect under the weight of my helmet. Every exposed piece of my skin felt gritty with sand. I just wanted to get to where we were going and get there soon.

We rumbled down the road for a time, then Hernandez and I watched as brake lights flashed from the lead vehicle to the next until we were at a complete stop. King was at the front of our column; Dowdy was in the last vehicle. There was radio contact between those two vehicles, but not to anyone beyond the reach of our short-range radios. They must have exchanged some information over the radio because we watched as Captain King and Dowdy got out of their trucks and conferred. Then they made their way down the line from vehicle to vehicle.

King stepped up onto the running board of our truck by Hernandez's open window. "You guys doing okay?" he asked.

"Yes, sir," we said.

"We're about to go into the city. Be prepared for snipers. Stay alert. Stay together."

"Okay," we said.

He stepped off the truck, and he and Dowdy moved down the row, talking to everyone.

We didn't know what we would find in the city. I figured it had to be safe to go through there or they wouldn't have planned our route into the town. If it wasn't safe, they wouldn't make us, the mechanics and cooks and support personnel, go through without protection, right? I looked at Hernandez to see if he had any sign of worry on his face. He didn't seem overly nervous. He just looked tired, dog tired, and ready to be done with this mess.

One after the other, we restarted our engines and crept forward on the road. It wasn't long before we came to an intersection, and it was here that we made the second wrong turn. We should have turned left to follow Route Blue, which would have taken us west and around the outside of the city. Instead, we went straight ahead, over a bridge, over the Euphrates River, and into the heart of the city.

Dawn had finally arrived and the early sun gave everything a pale orange glow. Of course, at the time I had no idea that we had missed our turn or that we were headed in the wrong direction, but from the start of our trip into that city, I instinctively knew that something was very wrong. The bridge was high and long and curved a bit as we headed toward what was obviously a medium-size city. There wasn't much in the way of suburbs, just suddenly a city surrounded by desert. The closer we got, the more we could see the tall buildings and narrow streets, plenty of places for bad people to hide.

Alarms went off in my head when we passed an Iraqi checkpoint. Iraqi men in civilian clothes and carrying weapons were standing at the checkpoint. A car had been parked across the road to partially block traffic. We simply drove around it. The men watched us drive by and actually waved at us.

We had been briefed that it was possible that some of the Iraqis would retain their weapons partly because they needed them for their own protection and it would be impossible to disarm them immediately upon our arrival. So we drove by these armed men as if we knew where we were going. I didn't wave back at them.

There was nothing about this trip that felt right. I couldn't believe we were driving into a city, a long line of supply trucks, a bunch of maintenance soldiers with M16s and little else. What possible reason could there be for us to go into that city? This is the moment that haunts me. Should I have refused to go farther? Should we have stopped and questioned what we were doing? If I had, would my friends still be alive?

I kept my mouth shut and got progressively more nervous as we moved slowly through the city at convoy speed, about twenty to thirty miles an hour. The streets were narrow, the roads pot-holed and cracked. The buildings that lined the streets were crumbling and lopsided, as if they stood only because they were holding each other up. It was like driving into a canyon with multistory buildings towering over us. Everything looked decayed and in need of maintenance. A stray donkey trotted away from the loud rumble of our trucks. A few goats munched on the meager grass they could find in narrow areas between buildings. We passed broken-down pushcarts and run-down garages with the odd Mercedes sedan shining inside. No one was on the streets. I wondered if they were deserted because it was so early or if the residents knew we were coming and were all hiding inside. The deserted streets really freaked me out. I felt eyes on us from the windows. There was no way there could be no people around in a city this size. I knew they were hiding, watching us.

At some point, someone must have finally decided we might be headed in the wrong direction because the column of vehicles began to turn around. *No shit,* I was thinking. *Let's turn around and get the hell out of here.*

Up ahead, I watched as everyone attempted to make a U-turn. That was no small thing, considering the trucks we were driving, the number of vehicles we had, and the size of the road. It took a while for all of us to turn around, some of us having to go forward, then back, then forward again to reverse the direction of the huge trucks. The time it took some vehicles to make the U-turn opened up distance between vehicles. By the time we were all headed back down the road we had just driven over, I couldn't see the lead vehicle anymore. We headed straight for a while, speeding up to re-form our tight group. Not long after that we stopped.

"What the hell is going on?" I asked, knowing Hernandez didn't have the answer.

I didn't like that we had stopped. Alarms were going off in my head. I knew we were being watched from all of the windows that towered over us. I felt trapped in there.

"Why are we stopping?" I wanted to know. "Let's go, let's just go."

I was feeling anxious and frustrated as I climbed down from the truck to pull security. I carried my M16 at port arms with my left hand supporting the barrel, my right wrapped around the trigger guard, my finger near the trigger. Hernandez stayed in the truck and I didn't blame him. He was exhausted. I moved to the front of the truck, where Private First Class Howard Johnson III and Private E-2 Ruben Estrella-Soto were pulling security by their truck. They strolled over to me and Johnson said, casual as can be, "What's up, Johnson?"

"Hey," I said.

"What's up, Hernandez?" Johnson said. "You're not getting out of the truck. Are you scared?" he asked, teasing him.

"Don't be scared," Estrella said. "We just gotta take care of this stuff right here."

I didn't understand what they were talking about. Take care of what? I learned later that some of the vehicles in our convoy had already taken fire. Someone had started shooting at us and I didn't even know it at that point. As if to confirm that things had changed, I saw Johnson and Estrella lock and load.

Lock and load. The only time I had ever been given that order was on a firing range. It is essentially the order to cock your weapon, to ensure a round is in the chamber and ready to fire. We wouldn't be firing at paper targets or pop-up silhouettes this time. The only reason to lock and load your M16 is if you need to get ready to kill someone. The two young soldiers, both of them so new to the Army, were cavalier about the whole thing. I exchanged a look with Hernandez through the windshield, then pulled back on the charging handle of my M16 and felt the round slip into the chamber. I thought about switching the safety off but decided to wait until I had something to shoot. I scanned the darkened windows of the buildings around us and wondered if there were weapons pointed at us already. My heart was flipping wildly in my chest.

As if the whole lock-and-load thing wasn't enough, I was beginning to worry about our fuel supply. The switch to change to our reserve tank had been malfunctioning and it wouldn't be long before we would either run out of gas or have to stop and siphon the fuel to the main tank. I didn't want to think about doing that in these streets.

Someone shouted at us to mount up.

"We gotta get outta here," they said. "This is for real!"

What was for real? What was going on? I didn't know, but I ran back and clambered into the truck and we took off again. We went straight for a time, then turned left, then right, then right again. The streets were narrow, though, so sometimes it took a while to maneuver the turn. The truck immediately in front of us was taking a long time to maneuver through the turn and we watched as the rest of the convoy was speeding away.

"Just go around them," I told Hernandez.

"Hey, they're going kind of fast," Hernandez said, seeing the growing distance between us and the rest of the convoy.

"Well, keep up," I said, my grip getting tighter on my weapon and my eyes peeled for anything to happen. The tension had suddenly ramped up and the vehicle in front of us was moving too slow. I had no idea that the vehicles that had passed us, the ones that had already made the turn, were already taking fire. We had the biggest trucks and it was taking us longer to make the turn. The slow speeds and the sitting and waiting were driving me crazy. I could see Pie as we drove past; she was shaking her head, the expression on her facing telling me she was thinking the same thing I was, that this was screwed up in a big way. I could see Dowdy sitting next to her, his brow knit in a serious expression.

I couldn't see the first vehicles of the convoy now; we were spread out, and anyway, most of them were around the corner from us. I saw that they had made yet another left turn to put us back on the main road and maybe headed back out of the city on the same road we had taken to enter this place. I was almost relieved at this prospect. We were getting out of there.

Hernandez made his turn and put pedal to the metal as we tried to catch up with the rest of the group. By the time we finally completed the turn, the folks doing the shooting were ready for us. We rounded a corner and I immediately started hearing the bullets pinging off our truck. It sounded like someone throwing rocks at us. It wasn't rocks. Those were bullets. People were trying to kill us.

"They're shooting at us," Hernandez shouted.

That was an understatement. At first it was just a few pings at a time, but then the noise became a constant barrage. Bullets were zipping by and pinging off the hood, the doors, everything, sounding like a hailstorm raining down on us. It was like we had run a gauntlet and we were at the tail end; our attackers were ready for us and they were pouring it on. Hernandez was trying to drive and duck out of the line of fire at the same time. I was amazed he kept us on the road as long as he did. Our windshield shattered. We sped forward, running for our lives, and came upon a dump truck that had been driven across the road to block our route.

"They're shooting at us from there," Hernandez said.

"I don't think so," I said. "You've got to go around it."

He swerved the truck to the left and tried to avoid the barricade that had been created with the huge truck and we fell into their trap. As they had planned, we avoided the dump truck but our huge truck quickly sank into the soft shoulder of the road and we weren't going any farther. We were stuck. We were screwed.

It was then that Pie's vehicle was hit with an RPG. I heard the explosion as the round from the rocket-propelled grenade hit them. In the next moment, they slammed into the back of our truck. Since Hernandez and I weren't moving, we felt the impact as if we had been hit with a rocket ourselves.

We were both thrown forward. I cracked my head a good one on the windshield frame and was grateful for my helmet. Hernandez was thrown against the steering wheel and it took a moment for us to shake ourselves and check our situation. Hernandez looked into his side-view mirror to see what had happened to Pie and the rest of them.

"Oh my God! It's the first sergeant," Hernandez said. "They're dead. They're all dead."

"No, that can't be the first sergeant," I said. I was operating under the hope that Dowdy would save our asses. He would come along, and we would get into his truck and we would all get out of there. I stretched across Hernandez to have a look for myself. One glance at the twisted wreckage and it was clear that rescue was not coming from them. Dowdy and my friend Pie, Lynch, and two others were also in the truck. Hernandez had been right. It looked like they were all dead.

"We have to get out of here," I said. The bullets were still flying and I was still hearing large explosions coming from up the road.

My head whipped around as I looked to see where all this fire was coming from. I saw a man coming at us from between two buildings. He was about three hundred meters away when I first saw him, a young guy wearing a white shirt and dark pants, his tennis-shoed feet kicking up wisps of sand as he ran toward us. He was carrying a pistol and I knew he would use it.

I flipped the selector switch on my M16 from safe to semiautomatic and raised my weapon to fire. My hands were shaking. I was good at long distances, had consistently hit the long targets on the range, but this was different. The man was moving, for one thing, coming right at me. But that wasn't what was different. He was aiming at me. This was a target that was aiming back, trying to kill me or one of my friends. Still, I didn't take too much time to think about it. I raised my weapon in his direction and fired. I saw the round hit the ground near him, and he took off in a sprint, ducking down, realizing someone was firing at him. He ran for cover in a crouched position and I didn't have time to try again. Rounds were raining down on us from the buildings, from people in the street, from everywhere. Thick black smoke was drifting at us from around the corner and I knew some of our trucks were already burning.

"We gotta get out of here." I screamed it this time.

We took a second to decide which side of the truck to climb out of, but neither option was better than the other. We decided to climb out on my side of the truck, Hernandez scooting across the seat and climbing down after me. As soon as we were out of the truck, I saw Miller running by.

"Miller!" I shouted, wanting some strength in numbers.

"I gotta go," he shouted. He ran at a sprint toward the front of the convoy. I learned later that he had climbed into one of the Humvees to man a .50-caliber machine gun in the turret of the truck. He manned that gun alone, taking out several of the men attacking us. He saw three men setting up a mortar position and was able to stop all of them before they killed any of our guys.

Shortly after that, Riley, Hernandez, and I crawled under our truck. Riley tried to fire my weapon, but it jammed. Hernandez's weapon jammed, too. Riley had already abandoned his useless weapon. Later, I would think about that thick green tape I had been instructed to wrap around my magazines. The hundred-mile-an-hour tape with the backing that was so sticky—it was tough to get it off your fingers when you touched it. Add the desert heat, and that thick tacky stuff would have coated the rounds in the magazines, causing them to fix tight in the bolt and stop them from moving up to be loaded. Riley tossed my useless weapon aside, and from later reports, you would think that all of our weapons had malfunctioned. The press reports seemed to blame us for the problems. Somehow it was our fault we had gotten lost. It was our fault that our weapons malfunctioned and that our radios didn't work. It was our fault we had been ambushed and captured.

But the press didn't say anything about our orders to use that damn tape. They didn't say anything about our attempts to repair radios that didn't work and they didn't say anything about how the TCP had abandoned us in the middle of the desert and, evidently, forgotten that we were out there.

They also didn't say anything about the way Miller and so

many others in the unit fought back. Yes, five of us were captured, eleven of us were killed, but most of us fought like hell and got away. I was shot. Hernandez was shot. A lot of my friends died. Johnson and Estrella, the two young soldiers I had spoken to only minutes before, had died. Every day of my captivity I wondered why they were killed and not me. Hell, I still wonder that.

22

Moving Around

The day after the prison was almost blown apart, I was woken up in the middle of the night and told we were moving. Moving. That meant I should be taking my things with me, but I didn't have things except for the small towel, the rag really, I had been given. I shoved the small towel into my pocket and stood silently as they tied my hands and blindfolded me.

I hadn't been asleep. The night so far had been shattered by constant gunfire. Gunfire, shouting, blasts going off left and right . . . I couldn't possibly sleep. I had been lying there, my eyes closed but in prayer, waiting for another explosion to bring the already damaged building down around my ears.

We were led outside and loaded into a truck. The minute we left the building it became obvious that the fight was right there, happening right around us. I couldn't see but I could smell the heat and coarseness of the air. I couldn't just hear rounds going off; I could hear the spent shells clattering to the ground. We took off through the night, the truck careening through the streets. We were jostled around in our seats.

They were driving fast in an attempt to outrun the bullets. Rounds zipped and splattered all around us. Automatic weapons fire was coming from opposite sides of the road, almost as if they were shooting at each other from opposing sidewalks—it was that close. On one side were Iraqis and on the other had to be Americans; which side was which was impossible to know, but the fighting was intense, unceasing. Shots came from one side, then the other, single shots but mostly the rapid bleat of weapons at full automatic.

I squeezed my eyes tightly shut behind my blindfold. Then a huge explosion went off right in front of the vehicle and we swerved recklessly around it, almost knocking me out of my seat. The tension in the truck was high. We all knew, prisoners and guards alike, that we were a target. Even if we weren't, we could stumble into something that would kill us all. I clenched my teeth and prayed and hoped for the best.

It was a relief to arrive safely at our destination until I saw the place. When my blindfold was removed, I was standing in a dirty little room that was empty save for a straight-backed chair. The walls were tiled in a dull yellow color. The place felt strange, so unlike the previous cell. The color didn't feel right and there was a small puddle of water in the corner of the room as if the roof leaked.

They sat me in the chair and left me there for a while. When one of the guards came back, he handed me my old bedroll. Gone was my comfortable hospital bed. I unrolled that thin mattress on the dirty floor and felt dread at the thought of lying on it. The whole place gave me the creeps. There were still battles going on around us, much more intense than they had been in the other prison. I sat there wondering what would happen next, listening to the thump of grenades or mortars going off and much of the firing sounding almost as if it were coming from the same building we were in.

I wondered why they would move us from a building that was falling apart around our ears to this place in the middle of a battle-field, when it dawned on me that this might have been exactly their intention. If we were killed in the fighting, if a stray bomb or errant attack happened and we were killed, they could blame it on America.

"You can't keep us here," I heard Williams saying loudly. "This place is unsanitary. This is against the Geneva Convention. You can't keep us here."

Williams kept it up, going on and on about the conditions. I was shocked at his demands. Did he think they would send in a cleaning crew to make it better?

"This is it. This is good," one of the guards said. "Better than most Iraqis." If that was true, I hated to think about what they were living in.

Fierce battles raged around us the entire day and night. I cowered on that thin mattress, worried that at any moment one of the bombs would find our building. The entire structure shook and rattled all night long. The telltale scream of an approaching explosion followed by the thump of the impact continuously vibrated through the walls and floor.

I must have slept a little because I had a dream that was becoming familiar. Before I joined the Army, I'd become entangled with a man who was married at the time. There was no way I could allow myself to get involved with this married man, but there was no denying the strong attraction between us and it took me a long time to forget about him. The man, I'll call him Martin, was a Marine when I met him. Some of my long nights in my prison cell I dreamed about Martin. I dreamed that he would lead a team of Marines to come rescue me and take me home.

That night, in the filthy house, in the quiet neighborhood where it was unlikely anyone would find us, Martin would do the impossible. He would find us and get me out of that hellhole.

Of course, the rescue was just a dream, and the next day, bleary from lack of sleep, I was taken to another room, where there was a bed. The familiar face of the man serving as my nurse was some comfort. With little communication he came in and gave me my antibiotics. The IV catheter on my hand was beginning to bother me. It had been in for several days and the site was getting sore to the touch. The nurse removed the catheter and tried to reinsert it in my other hand but wasn't successful. It hurt and I shouted out in pain.

Any time I displayed discomfort, everyone got nervous. The guys started shouting, wanting to know what was wrong, and the nurse got nervous and afraid he would get in trouble. His nervousness didn't help the situation and he was never able to get the catheter reinserted. I was relieved when he finally gave up. The smooth-talking doctor came and gave me a cursory examination, telling me I was healing fine.

I had my own doubts about that. Despite being able to shuffle along, my legs still screamed in agony every time I put weight on them. The wounds on my left leg seemed to be closing, but there was something seriously wrong inside because the pain wasn't going away. I suspected a broken bone, and I would find out later that I was right. My ankle, apparently, had been broken. Things were healing after a fashion. The open sores weren't bleeding as much as they had in the past, but that pain wasn't going away.

The wounds in my right leg were still open and festering. They didn't look like raw meat anymore, but they didn't look healthy either. The open sores weren't closing and my foot wasn't functioning the way it should. I felt sharp piercing pain with every step. As it turns out, my Achilles tendon had been shattered and the clean bandages the doctors applied weren't going to do a thing to fix that problem.

I was left alone in the room for a time, then several Iraqi men walked in. They looked surprised and not very happy to see me. I tried to keep my eyes down, hoping I would escape too much notice. They had AK-47s strapped to their chests and held loosely in their hands. Their faces were grimy, their clothes dusty, and every one of them looked bone weary. I figured the weapons they were carrying had contributed to all that gunfire I had heard the previous night. They must have been in the middle of the fight that had raged all night long. Their exhaustion was written on their faces and in the way they moved as if every gesture required painful effort. The men I was looking at were the enemy. They were the ones killing American soldiers, the ones American soldiers were trying to kill.

One of them was fair skinned and had very light-colored eyes. He could have walked down any street in Middle America and no one would suspect that he was an enemy.

They seemed to have come looking for a place to rest and recover. My presence wasn't welcome. They had been fighting and trying to kill Americans. They had spent hours trying to kill people like me. Maybe some of them had been killed by people like me. The man with the light-colored eyes opened the door and said something to someone down the hall. A guard came and I was ushered out of there. I wasn't sorry about leaving.

I was taken up a set of stairs to another room. I was happy to see that this one had a bed, too. I could hear the guys down the hall, so I was relieved to be closer to them. According to the Geneva Conventions, women prisoners are supposed to be kept separate from men, but it wasn't comfortable for me to be kept away from them. I felt isolated and vulnerable in my separateness.

The walls in this place were thin and I could hear that the men were able to talk to each other. Some of the conversation made me think some of them might be sharing rooms. Of course they were told to shut up, but they took every opportunity to push the limits, to see how far they could take things. They were prisoners but they weren't ever going to be passive about it. They wanted to make sure the guards understood there was still a lot of fight left in them despite their circumstances. I was constantly frightened for them every time they acted up, but I was proud of them, proud of their bravery.

The next day, after another night punctuated by battles raging around us, we were moved yet again. The pudgy guard with the reddish hair, along with the big flirt, the one who thought he should be my boyfriend, came in to prepare me for the move. Pudgy was carrying an AK-47 with multiple loaded magazines stuffed into the pockets of his vest. He had always been kind to me, and it was a shock to see him loaded for war, but considering the neighborhood we were in and the fact that we were going out into that combat zone, I guess I shouldn't have been surprised.

The flirt went to tie my hands, but Pudgy stopped him, saying not to bother. They waited to blindfold me until we got downstairs, but even after that, I stumbled and knocked my leg against something that shot fiery pain to my wounds. They kept the blindfold off so that I could walk without hurting myself. We got outside, and for the first time, I saw the truck they had been using to move us around in.

It was an ambulance. A large white box with a red crescent moon symbol painted on the side. No wonder we had driven through those battles without being blown to bits. They crowded five of the men together on a litter along one wall of the ambulance. I was put in a seat behind a guard. I figured they stuck me there because of my injured legs. Miller was put in a seat behind me, and the flirt sat next to him.

Once I was in the vehicle, they put my blindfold back on, but seeing the men had already been a shock. They all looked ragged as they shuffled out of the building. Most of them had facial hair growing in and they looked thin and tired with their blindfolds on and tied hands.

The ride was uneventful, but this time, when my blindfold came off, I was definitely in another cell in a genuine prison or maybe a city jail. This cell was even smaller than the first one, with a barred opening high up in the wall and another small barred opening that served as a peephole in the cell door. The one improvement was that there was carpet on the floor. The carpet didn't improve the comfort my bedroll provided or improve my sleep. The fighting and dying were still going on outside and I was sure I would never grow accustomed to the shock of the building rattling around me.

One of the guards had always been particularly kind to me. He was an older man, short, with a thin mustache. He told me he had eleven children. Eleven! He seemed sorry for me and went out of his way to be kind. When I knocked on my cell door in the morning to ask if I could be taken to the bathroom, the kind old guard was there and had obviously slept curled up on the floor outside my door. I was surprised by it and wondered why he felt the need to do that. Was there some danger in this place I wasn't aware of?

He walked me down the hall, showing great patience for my slow, painful pace, and I had time to look around to get familiar with my new surroundings. My cell was part of a row of doors arrayed along one wall that faced an open, grassy courtyard. My wall was one side of a complete square that surrounded the courtyard. I could tell other prisoners were in the jail by the way the guards walked down the rows of cells and looked in the windows of the doors. I wondered if they were all Iraqi and what they had done to end up in this place.

We walked down to the end of the row of cells and entered a large bathroom with several stalls like a familiar barracks latrine. I didn't have much time to check it out. I did what I needed to do and returned to my cell.

My cell was a very dark little room. Very little natural light came through my small window and there wasn't any electric light. I sat there most of the day praying, thinking about home, wondering when someone was going to get us the heck out of there.

I started to allow myself to imagine what it would be like to go home. How it would feel to see Janelle again. I wondered what the media were saying about us and tried to imagine how life would take shape again once I got home. I sang my song, "Amazing Grace," and waited and thought and waited.

Sometime later, I was taken out of my cell. The guard didn't say where we were going; I simply followed his instructions to come along. It made me nervous not to know what was coming. He opened a door and motioned for me to go in. There was a man standing next to a chair. I had never seen him before and I wondered what he wanted. What he said was about the last thing in the world I would have expected.

"I am a dentist," he said.

A dentist. Bombs were going off. Bullets were flying, I'm a prisoner of war, and this guy wanted to check out my teeth!

He told me to sit down and open up and I wondered if I should mention that my tongue was pierced. I was still wearing the small flesh-colored stud in my tongue I had put on when we left Camp Virginia. But he just checked out my teeth, and since he didn't say anything about the tongue piercing, I didn't say anything.

"You must brush every day," he said.

He gave me a toothbrush and some toothpaste.

You have got to be kidding, I thought. *Like I don't have plenty of other things to worry about.*

"When you go back to America, your teeth will be okay," he said.

When I go back to America? Did that mean we were leaving soon? But I couldn't get my hopes up. I was taken back down to the communal bathroom, where I could actually brush my teeth for the first time since we had been captured. I have to admit it felt wonderful, but I still didn't understand why it was so important for us to see a dentist.

I was taken back to my cell and I listened as the guys were taken out, one by one, to see the dentist. They each made their own comments about the surprising nature of the visit. A dentist? It just didn't seem right.

23

Thinking

I could hear the guys talking. There must have been an empty cell between me and their rooms, because I could hear them, but they didn't seem to hear me. I could hear Williams talking sometimes. He would ask everyone how they were doing and they would wait their turn, then report, "I'm okay." I tried to chime in but they didn't acknowledge my response.

The hours of the day dragged on. Sleep was elusive. Between the sounds of war outside and the complete lack of things to do inside, I just couldn't turn my brain off to get rest. I started exercising just to work off some energy so that I could sleep. I did crunches, flutter kicks, and leg lifts, the huge bandages on my legs acting as makeshift extra weight. I couldn't do push-ups. The pressure on my legs would have been excruciating. When I had left home, I had it in my head that I could maybe lose some weight on the deployment, never realizing that I would be reduced to gruel and rice and an occasional piece of chicken. If anything good came out of this captivity, maybe I would drop twenty pounds. I knew I was losing weight already, so I did crunches and flutter kicks and hoped to see some results.

Despite my exercise routine, I found myself playing back the video of the ambush in my head over and over again. I berated myself for not putting up a fuss about driving into the city when I knew in my gut it had been the wrong thing to do. I saw Lori's bloody face and the first sergeant's battered body. I wondered about Jessica and everyone else in the unit we couldn't account for.

I kept hearing the sounds, feeling my panic and the pain of being shot. I thought about the man I tried to shoot. I had missed. He had been far away, but it was a distance I normally hit during target practice. I wondered what I would be feeling if I had killed him. I wondered if my missing him meant that he killed others in my unit.

As the hours wore on, I would listen to the men as they kept up their banter back and forth.

"Hey, Ron," Williams said. "What are you doing?"

"I'm getting ready to go out on a date," Young said. "What are you doing?"

"I'm building a house, brick by brick."

They were exercising their imaginations, using their time to construct images of what they would do if they weren't here. I guess I was doing the same thing, only my constructs seemed much more superficial! I was thinking about going to movies and dropping twenty pounds, when these guys were trying to do something constructive with their time. I felt bad. I felt shallow!

Still, hearing them talk made me feel better, made me feel as if I wasn't alone. They kidded each other, talked badly about the guards, the prison. The guards yelled at them, "Shut up! Shut up!" But they ignored them and continued to push the limits, to see how far they could go.

For lunch one day, along with our bowl of rice, we got two

cucumbers! I ate one immediately and kept the second one for later. It was rare to get fresh vegetables and chomping into a cucumber wasn't something I would normally do, but that green piece of nutrition tasted pretty damn good.

We only spent two nights in that prison or jail or whatever it was. The third day, during broad daylight, the nurse came in fully loaded for fighting. I'd never seen him with a weapon, but he not only had a weapon, he was carrying extra magazines and I almost didn't recognize him. He pantomimed to me to roll up my bedroll. I had my extra cucumber in my pocket and that, along with the thin mattress, was all I needed to take with me.

The nurse blindfolded me and walked me slowly out to the van. I was petrified. We had never moved during the day. We had never done anything outside of the prisons during the day and the nurse had never been armed before. I had never carried my own bedroll. Was this just a ruse to make me think I was moving when I was really going to my death? Was I about to be executed?

Your mind can do some serious gymnastics when you're scared. Mine was working a mile a minute as they loaded me into the truck. I couldn't see, but I was loaded into my familiar seat and I could picture in my head what was happening since I had seen it all before. The men were loaded on the litter, Miller was seated behind me, the flirt sitting next to him. When we were all inside the truck, we took off and drove for a long time. No one was shooting at us this time, which was good, since we drove for about an hour, maybe longer.

This time, when they took my blindfold off, we were in a house. It was obviously someone's home. I was pushed into a chair, and I looked around. It looked like the library of someone's home with lots of books crammed onto bookshelves, a large desk, thick carpets on the floor, a coatrack by the door.

Why would they take us to someone's house?

A man came in and it appeared as if this was his house, his office. He seemed angry when he told the nearest guard to put the blindfold back on me and that made me doubly nervous. They take me to someone's home and the guy doesn't want to be recognized?

Not to mention that we were no longer in a proper prison, no longer in a logical place to search for us if anyone was doing such a thing. Now we were in someone's house, a house among millions, and it made me feel a little helpless. My hopes for rescue seemed impossible.

24

Unwanted

I sat waiting in the office, wearing the blindfold, listening to the guards move furniture around. They seemed to be emptying rooms of furniture in preparation for us. Eventually I was taken to one of the rooms and seated in a chair. I could peek under the blindfold to see a blue-and-white tile floor and little else. The door opened again and two of the guys were brought in.

GREAT! I thought. *I'll be with the men now.*

But it was not to be. They moved the men in, then came for me and moved me to another room, where I was left alone again. They left the men, three to a room, but I was alone. I hated all of this separation. My room was small and had a large picture window. The guards closed the curtains but that didn't erase the vision of all that glass. With the bullets and bombs flying around outside, the prospect of so large a window made me a bit nervous. Since I could still barely walk on my own, I figured they put me in the room because I was the least likely to break the glass and make a run for it.

Run. Ha. As if!

I settled down on my bedroll and listened to the fighting going on outside. Someone in the street was firing an AK-47, the popping of the rounds sounding like it was right outside the house. The small automatic weapon was totally outgunned by what responded.

The thirty-millimeter cannon on an A-10 Warthog, or a Hog as it's sometimes called, makes a unique and unmistakable sound. The aircraft, designed for close air support, can carry a variety of bombs, but the cannons on board can fire almost four thousand rounds a minute. It sounds like something out of a science-fiction movie, like a long deep blast from a foghorn on a large ship only with a much darker purpose to the sound. The Hog streaks across the sky raining destruction on tanks with its armor-piercing bullets.

I didn't know what the sound was at the time. First I heard the AK-47 *pop, pop, popping.* Then, suddenly, a loud braying echoed off the houses in the area and shattered the sky. It went on for several seconds, streaking across the sky from a distance, then going overhead and away.

What the hell was that? I thought, unconsciously ducking with the knowledge that whatever it was, it brought danger. If I was frightened, I could only imagine what that little dude out there with his AK-47 was feeling. He was probably doing what anyone would have done under the circumstances—turning tail and running for his life.

The hours of the day dragged on endlessly. Around the house, I could hear kids playing in the street. I couldn't believe any parent would allow their child to be outside with so much war going on. It made me think of Janelle and of my niece, and I could not believe that those children outside weren't locked up tight and safe from all of the fighting. This neighborhood, wherever the house was, was not a safe place. Not for children, not for anyone.

Again it was a restless night with rounds going off all around us, explosions shaking the ground and the house. The glass in the window rattled on its hinges and I couldn't get away from imagining it shattering and raining down on top of me.

I was petrified. I almost pounded on the door and begged to be allowed to spend the night with the guys. I didn't want to be alone. Having someone near would have helped calm my nerves, but I didn't knock. I huddled, wide-awake and frightened, alone in my small room.

The next day, the doctor came to see me, apologizing for not having come the day before.

"I was in a car accident," he said. "I rolled my car three times."

"Are you okay?" I asked him.

"Yes, yes, but the car is not."

A man can live in a war zone, dodge bullets daily, and end up nearly getting killed in a regular old car accident.

He examined me. The wounds on my left leg had almost closed completely, but it was still excruciating to walk on and I knew there was something wrong inside that wasn't going to fix itself. To look at it from the outside, it looked fine, but it wasn't healed, and I wondered if the doctor knew that but wasn't willing to do anything more about it. The right leg was worse. He removed the walking cast and then took out the stitches, but the wound was still wide open, a gaping, raw hole in my flesh that didn't look healthy. It still hurt and didn't feel like it was getting any better, but the optimistic doctor wasn't bothered by this. He put clean bandages on my foot and replaced the walking cast, saying, "You are doing very, very well. They are healing very nicely."

I kept my mouth shut.

The best part about being in the house was that I was allowed to take a shower. How glorious it was! There was a proper bathroom with a regular shower, tiles, and a sink. There wasn't a mirror but I wasn't too excited about seeing myself anyway. They still had a squat toilet but one couldn't expect to have everything.

By this time in my captivity, my T-shirt had ceased to be useful as a substitute for toilet paper. I had taken to using wads of cotton from my cast. It didn't go down the drains well, tended to clog things up, but I didn't care. If they weren't going to give me proper toilet paper, then I wasn't going to worry about their plumbing system. I needed to use something for the job, so I used what was available.

In the late afternoon, the kind little man who had slept outside my door came in apologizing.

"I'm so sorry, so sorry." He was holding a blindfold and gesturing that he needed to put it on me. That had to mean we were moving again. I shrugged and told him okay and allowed myself to be blindfolded. I could hear the men being rounded up, tied, blindfolded, and shuffled down the halls and into the waiting truck. We climbed into our familiar seats and took off again.

No one wanted us. We drove for hours, stopping at several different places where conversations would take place. We could hear the guards having discussions with people. We couldn't understand what they were saying, but it was pretty obvious that we were being turned away.

I thought back to the man in that house, the one who'd wanted my blindfold put back in place. He was probably the home owner and had been reluctantly talked into taking us. One night was all he could stand and then we had been booted out. We had to be dangerous property, deadly contraband, for any of these men to be caught with and no one wanted the responsibility.

We were turned away repeatedly, and at one point, we stopped and pulled over to the side of a road while the driver got out and spoke to someone. We sat there for a long time—long enough for the guards to get bored and to even let us pull up our blindfolds.

We sheepishly looked around at each other. I looked at Hernandez, who seemed more tired and disheveled than the last time I had seen him in our truck. It was the first time I could get a good look at all of the men and the first time Williams and Young had ever met me.

"Are you okay?" Williams said.

"I'm okay. You?" I said.

"We're okay," he said, looking around at everyone.

Hudson and Williams had a tie going for the most facial hair. I was surprised at how tall Young was. He had to be well over six feet, kind of hunched over on that uncomfortable litter.

Three men were in the truck with us serving as our guards: the kind old man, a larger, cocky-looking guy who frightened me with his dark and angry stare, and one man who wore a suit jacket and carried a pistol instead of an automatic weapon like the rest of them.

Suit Jacket turned and pointed to Young. "I have seen your family on television, and your family and your family." He pointed to all of us and said he had seen our families on television. Then he pointed to Williams. "I have not seen your family. Why is that? Why no family?"

Williams shrugged. "I have a wife and kids," he said. "I would like to go home to them."

"I have big family," the kind man said. "I have two wives and eleven children." Then he looked at me. "You should stay in Iraq. Marry a nice Iraqi man. Marry a good Muslim man. You stay."

Everyone laughed, including me. He was smiling and nodding as if this were the most natural thing in the world. The last thing I would ever consider was to stay in this place, a place that, so far, had shown me nothing but pain and abject terror. I would never consider his proposal, but then he kept repeating it and the other guards agreed with him and then it wasn't so funny to me anymore. I hoped they weren't serious.

We continued to sit and wait. The guards would get out, go talk to someone, come back, and we waited for them to figure out what to do with us. The cocky-looking guy with the dark expression told us his brother had been killed by an American bomb. He didn't seem angry but the event explained his dark expression. I knew I would be feeling a similar emotion if the tables had been turned.

The dark man said something disparaging about President Bush, expecting to start some kind of political discussion.

"Bush's children aren't here," Williams said.

That seemed to put an end to that discussion.

We waited. It was obvious that if we had originally been in the custody of the Iraqi Army, we weren't in their custody anymore. Maybe these guys had been soldiers at one point. I had seen the nurse and the kind old man in uniform, but they weren't acting as if they were affiliated with any army now. We didn't know who these guys were, or what they had planned, and it appeared as if they didn't have much of a plan.

Maybe I was a little slow on the realization, but it finally dawned on me that if they didn't find a place to take us, someone who would agree to hide us, they might just take us out to the desert and have done with us. Killing us and leaving us was one of their alternatives. I looked around at the men, and we didn't need to talk about it. I could see that they had all come to the same conclusion. The longer we waited, the more I began to worry.

Eventually, they took us to a place that looked just like a lock-and-leave storage facility. Tiny rooms, no more than six or seven feet long, maybe five feet wide, with heavy metal doors and small peepholes. The cells were so tiny, it reminded us of a place people would rent to store their unnecessary things. The guards put the men two to a room and I was given one to myself. I could barely lie flat in mine, the bedroll going from wall to wall. They put the two tallest men, Young and Hudson, together and I knew they only did that to mess with them, to make them uncomfortable in that one tiny cell.

There were no windows. A lightbulb dangled from the center of the ceiling and bathed the room in a bright light. The glare was annoying, but if I turned it off, the room would have been in total darkness; the only natural light came from under the door. The lack of windows made the air thick and dusty feeling. It was cooler in the darkened room but heavy with stale air.

The only saving grace to the place was that the walls were thin and for the first time I was able to converse with the men in the rooms near mine. Maybe it was the ability to talk to them, or it could have been sheer relief that we weren't going to be killed and dumped in the desert, but hearing their voices and being included in the conversation made me feel as if I were a true member of the group and that was very comforting.

"You gotta stop singing that song," Young told me. "Every time you sing 'Amazing Grace' it breaks my heart."

"The words to that song never hit me until you started to sing it here," Williams said.

"Sorry," I said. "It just brings me comfort."

"It's okay. I understand," he said.

We continued to go back and forth, talking and joking with each other, sometimes getting out of hand, our voices and laughter growing in volume. The guards would come around to tell us to shut up. We would be quiet for a time and then start up again. It was food for my soul.

It dawned on me that much of the day I hadn't heard any rounds going off. Nothing was exploding and no one was shooting at us. It might have been one reason why we were able to relax a bit and actually laugh with each other. There wasn't a necessity to cringe and duck, the instinctive reactions to the violent noises of the war.

At one point, a man in uniform came to my door. He opened it and stood there, staring at me. The guys could hear him open my door and I could almost feel them tense up, straining to hear what was going on, knowing that someone was at my door. I didn't like the looks of the guy. He was pudgy, with a thin mustache, wearing a black military beret and a brown khaki uniform. His dark eyes raked over me.

"Are you married?" he asked me, an angry, almost accusatory tone to the question.

"No."

"Children?"

"Yes."

He stood there for a long moment continuing to stare. Finally he shut the door and left and I wondered what that had been about. Then I heard Williams through the wall.

"Shana, from now on, if anyone asks, you are married," he said.

"Okay," I said, understanding the wisdom of this advice. I thought about the conversation with the guards earlier that day and their suggestion that I marry an Iraqi man. That combined with the encounter with the strange man standing in my door was enough to give me fresh worries. I had been separated from the men for the most part. What if they simply handed me over to some man to keep? Would they force me to stay here as someone's wife? The idea was too awful to contemplate and I tried to not think about it.

The next morning, Williams decided it was time to play a joke on the guards.

"What?" I said. "Are you crazy?"

He instructed us to roll up our bedrolls so that when the guards came, we could be standing there all ready to move again. They had been moving us so much we wanted to let them know their predicament wasn't lost on us. We didn't even have time to execute the joke properly since the guards arrived then, to tell us we were moving again.

This time they put us in the truck and we stayed in it the entire day. We loaded up sometime in the morning and it wasn't until the middle of the night that we arrived at our destination. They seemed to know where they were going at least. There wasn't as much stopping, no long conversations about what to do with us. They simply drove. At one point, we pulled over and all of the guards got out of the truck, leaving us alone. By this time, the guys had figured out how to get their hands untied, and we could all push the sleep masks they used as blindfolds up onto our foreheads. We were looking around, wondering what was going on.

"They're sitting right over there at a table. Some kind of restaurant," I told the men.

"You're kidding," Young said.

"Nope, just sitting there, all comfortable. They're having tea!"

We were on a busy street in a city. It wasn't Baghdad. I could tell from the sounds of the road that we had left the city some time ago. Williams and Young were discussing what direction we were traveling in and they decided it had to be north.

"They could just keep going and drop us off in Turkey or something," Young said.

"They could just drop us off at the nearest U.S. base," I said.

"What are we doing here, sitting out in the open like this?" I didn't like it. I felt exposed.

"Calm down, Shana," Williams said.

"What if we just take off?" Young suggested. "We could escape."

We all thought about that for a few seconds and discussed the alternatives. Hernandez and Hudson with their beards and olive complexions could maybe pass for Iraqi, but we had been stopped at checkpoints all along the road. A single stop at a checkpoint meant capture since none of us spoke Arabic. I could maybe be hidden by a burka, but one look at me, one look at any of the rest of us, Young especially, and someone would raise the alarm.

Williams was the voice of reason. "We just better sit tight," he said. And we agreed.

The guards must have heard us talking because suddenly the rear door of the ambulance was opened. We all slipped our hands back into the restraints and pushed our blindfolds back down. Williams either forgot or just didn't bother to push his blindfold down. I could peek under the fabric of my own mask and I saw the dark-looking guard staring at Williams as if surprised to see his eyes revealed and staring back at him. The guard reached over and pushed Williams's blindfold down, then rapped him on the head with his knuckles as if to say, *Wear it down and keep it down.*

Then the guard shut the ambulance door and left.

It was laughable. Things were getting awfully casual and I wondered where this was all going.

Finally, they finished their tea break and we started the journey again. An hour later we arrived at our next stop. When they brought us inside and removed our blindfolds, it appeared as if we were in a house again. The best part, at least for me, was that we were all in the same room. It was a large room with an off-white tile floor and rough, sickly-looking green plaster walls. It seemed like an older house but it was clean and comfortable. Our sleeping mats had been arranged around the room, six of them for the men lined against one wall and one for me on the opposite side in a corner. A small tea table was near my sleep mat along with a small Igloo ice chest and one glass.

The people who took our blindfolds off and untied our hands were totally new faces to us. One guy looked like a teenager, maybe seventeen. There was an older, distinguished-looking guy, maybe the teenager's dad, and one guy who looked like a body-builder, short and stocky with a large barrel chest.

The bodybuilder handed me a glass of water.

"It will be okay," he said. "Drink this and we will bring you food."

The water was ice cold and refreshing and it was great to be in the same room with the men. Something had changed. Our familiar guards were gone and these new people seemed different, not like military people at all. They seemed tentative, unsure of what to do. It made me nervous not to understand why things had changed so drastically.

"What the hell is going on, Dave?" I asked.

"I don't know," Williams said. We all looked at each other try-ing to figure out the change in our situation.

They brought us pieces of chicken that had been fried, rice, and hot tea. It smelled good, but I couldn't eat much. After our meal, we took turns getting cleaned up in the bathroom down the hall. I lay on my mat that night, not sure I would be able to sleep. The heavy breathing and snores from the men were reassuring. I slept, grateful to not be alone.

The next day, when they brought us breakfast, the bodybuilder said something that put hope in my heart.

"You will go home soon," he said. "Rumsfeld will come for you soon."

I didn't say anything in response. I didn't know what to think, but as soon as he left, we started speculating.

"Do you think the war is over?" I asked. When things got confusing, I automatically asked Chief Williams what he thought. He was the leader; he was smart and seemed in command of his situation and ours. I felt safer in his company and in the company of the rest of the men, so I sought his help to clarify things for me. In this case, we hadn't heard any bombing for a couple of days. Did he think the war was over?

"I don't know," Williams said. "But I'm not going to believe it until it happens."

As the day wore on, the teenage boy added his voice to the hopeful information. "You will go home very soon," he said.

I didn't want to get my hopes up, but it was hard not to start thinking about the possibility of sleeping in my own bed, of having a shower, of getting my hair done and wearing something other than the filthy pajamas. I wanted to see my family, to hold Janelle, to move about on my own free will. I tried to follow the advice and not believe the promises until we knew something concrete, but it was very difficult not to grasp at any slim ray of hope. It might have been that the words of encouragement were meant to ensure we stayed calm and didn't try to escape, but if we were going home soon, I was ready for it.

25

House Hunting

The house wasn't much of an improvement in accommodations, but the food was definitely much better. Breakfast that first day was tasty, a nice plate of crackers, cheese, and a pot of tea. No more of that horrible gruel. One of the men brought in the food and seemed pleased by our appreciation of its tastiness.

By this time, some of the guys were having stomach problems; the food or the water was causing discomfort. Williams spoke to the older man to see if something could be done for them.

We spent the day quietly talking, sleeping—waiting to see what would happen next. There wasn't anything to do but to sit idly and wait. Waiting is something you grow accustomed to in the military, but waiting is always hard even when you know what you're waiting for. It is four times as hard when there doesn't seem to be any purpose for the waiting. Sitting. Talking. Waiting.

Suddenly the door was thrown open and a large man appeared, wearing flowing white robes and a long white kaffiyeh, the traditional Arab headdress, billowing wide as he came charging into our room. He was dark skinned, with a thick beard, and carried an automatic weapon, holding it casually in his hand as if it were harmless. He swayed a bit and his eyes seemed unfocused. Every face in the room turned to him as he came in and we wondered what he wanted.

"Fuck Iraq!" he said, spittle flying everywhere.

We stared at him in shock. I looked at the guys, checking for their reaction. Everyone was frozen, wondering what would happen next. Young jumped up and said, "Bathroom, WC," as his excuse to leave the room. He wisely left, skirting around the man and avoiding the awkward intrusion. I wondered if he was also on a mission to let someone know that a crazy man had just entered our room.

The Arab paced around, the weapon swinging wildly in his hand. We ducked when the arc of the weapon pointed in our direction and kept our eyes glued to him, knowing this guy was unstable and there was no way to tell what he might do next.

"Fuck Iraq," he repeated, more angry this time and searching for some reaction from us.

After several seconds of his wild pacing, the older man rushed in, wrapping his arms around the crazed Arab, leading him out of the room.

"It's okay. It's okay," the older man said to us, motioning for us to stay calm and seeming apologetic. He quickly closed the door behind him.

I let out my breath and looked around at everyone. We chuckled nervously, wondering what the heck that was all about.

I had plenty of time that day to think about the promises of freedom. I tried not to, but there was nowhere else for my mind to turn. Were they looking for us? Why hadn't the Special Forces come to get us out? Or was it true what our captors had hinted at before? Would we simply be released? Maybe someone was negotiating for our freedom.

Later that evening, the familiar routine began yet again. The older man came in, told us to stand up. We held our hands out to be tied and the bodybuilder let us know he wasn't looking forward to moving us around. He grumbled his displeasure under his breath in a language we couldn't understand, but his attitude about what was happening was clear in his posture. He peered at Williams and switched to English.

"Hey," the bodybuilder said. "You drive." He tried to keep a serious face, but there was the hint of a smile there. He was kidding, but not really.

Williams stared at him, then shook his head. "Oh no," he said. "You take us to the Americans."

The man shook his head. "No, it's okay. You drive stick, right?" Now it was pretty obvious that he was joking, but Williams played along.

"No, I think you better drive," he said.

It was hard not to hope that this was it. This was our release. This was what they had promised. We were blindfolded and led out to the truck, and I was nervous with excitement, thinking soon we would be home, but after a very short trip in our familiar van, those hopes were dashed.

When my blindfold was removed, we were in what seemed like a newly built house. The room was large and clean, the sleep mats arrayed along the walls, and gratefully, I noticed my bedroll was in the same room as the men.

It was yet another house and another set of men taking care of us. There were a few moments of awkwardness as we looked around and decided which spot in the room we would claim as our own, all under the watchful eyes of the three new guards.

Once we made our sleeping spot selections, one of the men handed me a pillow and a blanket. As soon as the door was closed, the guys spoke up.

"Hey, you gotta cough one of those up," they complained collectively. I gave up the blanket but kept the pillow for myself.

We talked about the offer to drive ourselves away. "They're crazy," Williams said. "We're not going anywhere on our own. Either Americans come and get us, or they hand us directly over to the Americans."

He was right, of course. Who knew if they would suddenly change their minds once we were in the van and driving away? It could have been a setup. They could say we were shot trying to escape. They could say anything. It was better, smarter, for us to stay put and figure out what was going on, but it wasn't easy. Things seemed to be deteriorating. We didn't know why we were getting passed from one group to the next, didn't know if these were Iraqi soldiers, ordinary citizens, or some kind of insurgent group. And we didn't know if the next group that took charge of us would settle the whole thing by taking us out to the desert and shooting us.

After our meeting with the three new men who were watching us, execution seemed less likely. One of the men, who we referred to as the Captain, was a very thin man whose English, while broken, sounded as if he was educated. He was serious but kind, at least not threatening. They all seemed less threatening than our initial set of guards. The one we called the Major was pudgy with a thick mustache. He told us he had a wife and children. And one man we called Raymond because he looked exactly like Ray Romano, the comedian in the sitcom *Everybody Loves Raymond*. He looked so much like the actor that we all kind of stared at him, amazed at the similarity.

The men in charge of us now seemed like reluctant captors, as if they were confused about what to do with us. The Captain would talk to Williams, taking him out of the room for conversations. He revealed that they were all police officers, and while he never admitted that they didn't want us, it was clear they were making the best of an uncomfortable situation. They were kind. They were doing what they could.

They gave us a deck of cards and a chess set. We occupied our time playing games and talking. No one was banging on our doors telling us to shut up now.

Sometimes the games we played in the evenings were interrupted by power outages. Suddenly, the lights in the room would go out and there was no telling when they would come back on again. Most of the time we got along with the meager light that came in through the small windows, but other times, someone would bring us a kerosene lamp to use if we needed it.

Sitting in the semi-darkness, we would talk about our families, about the ambush, and about what we would do when we got home because now it seemed as if we might get home.

"If I don't make it home, I wonder if my daughter will even remember me," Miller said. His daughter was only a few months old when we deployed and I know she and his young wife were heavy on his mind the entire time.

"We're going to make it home," I told him.

"You think so?"

"I have to think that. Besides, I want to get home in time to see *The Matrix*," I said. The movie was scheduled to be released soon and the trailers had piqued my interest. I wanted to get home to see it. It had been over three weeks since we had been captured, and while I wanted to believe we would be going home soon, none of us had a clue what, if anything, was being done to find us.

Williams cautioned that if we made it back, we would be the subject of media attention for a time. Boy, was that a good prediction.

"Dave, do you think I'll be in *Jet* magazine?"

"Shana, I think you'll definitely be in *Jet* magazine," Williams said. By the time I made it home, I had already been written about in *Jet* twice over.

We talked endlessly about the ambush. What we saw, what we didn't see. Who we knew had died. Sergeant Walters had been second in charge of my section before we took off on this mission. He had predicted that he wouldn't be coming back. "I got a bad feeling about this, Johnson," he had said to me. "I don't think I'm going to make it."

I had assured him he was wrong, telling him he would be okay. Now I wondered what had happened to him. None of the guys had seen him during the battle, and as it turned out, what happened to Walters developed into a real mystery, with a lot of conflicting theories. I told the guys what Walters had predicted; in the end, his prediction had been right, although I didn't know it at the time.

"You know," Hernandez said quietly, "I don't like being shot at."

We looked at him, his innocent face serious about what he had just said. He was the baby of the group, only twenty years old.

"Yep, getting shot at kind of sucks," Miller said.

"None of us like it," Williams added.

"They were trying to kill us," Hernandez said.

It was true. People we didn't know had tried to kill us. There was a long pause as we all pondered what that meant. It didn't matter if we had children or were good people or had promising futures. These strangers had tried their best to kill us. You can try to rationalize that by saying we were soldiers in a war zone—what did we expect? But the reality is that someone had tried to kill *me*. Someone I didn't know and who didn't know me had tried to kill *me*. How can you not take that personally?

"But we're going to be okay," Williams said.

I hoped he was right. Things began to feel more hopeful any-way. The food was definitely better. In the morning, Raymond, the Major, and the Captain took us to another room, sat us down at a table, and served us an actual breakfast of crackers and cheese. They brought in a proper tea set, with a teapot and cups on a serving platter. It was all very civilized.

"You're a cook," Raymond said to me. "You serve."

I didn't like that idea much, but I served the men, pouring the light brown liquid into small teacups. Bits of leaves floated in the sweetened brew. It was pleasant to eat a meal seated at a table, as if things were normal and the world wasn't crazy outside.

The guards liked to talk to us over breakfast, telling us about their families, their children. The Captain would pull up a chair and sit, his legs crossed, casually leaning on the table.

"I have two wives," he said. "One became too influenced by the West and she was ruined. I had to get another wife. But I see what is out there," he said. "I have a satellite dish. I see your television."

Every chance they could, they told us we were going home. "Soon you will go home," they said. "Don't worry about it. You will be home soon."

I tried to take Williams's advice and not think about it, not get my hopes up, but it was nearly impossible to take my mind off the possibility of going home. What it would be like to sleep in a normal bed again, to flush a toilet, to have a shower. I had a vivid fantasy that I played in my head over and over again. I would eat a big juicy steak and a fat steaming baked potato, and drink a tall glass of beer, the sweat dripping down the glass. I visualized that meal so many times that I could almost taste it. I would lie on my mat at night, thinking about Janelle and my family and how it would feel to see them again. It was so frustrating. Going home felt close, like it could happen any moment.

None of us had seen a doctor in several days, not since the day we left the first house, which meant that our bandages were going unchanged. The bandages on my legs were getting very ragged and I was beginning to worry about infection, especially in my right leg since that wound still hadn't healed. I wondered why we were no longer under a doctor's care. It had seemed an important thing to our captors at one time.

That night, Raymond came to our room carrying a small bag filled with bandages and iodine. They looked like the kind of thing you would purchase from a local pharmacy, not like official supplies. I wondered if he had used his own money to buy the stuff. He removed the old bandages, which had grown filthy and blood soaked, and liberally applied iodine to the wounds in both my legs. My left leg still hurt like hell and the scars were red and raw but closed. The wounds on both sides of my right leg, on the ankle and the side that traveled up my calf, looked inflamed, a bright red that hurt just to look at.

Raymond gave Hernandez and Hudson the same kind treatment. As was the case with my legs, the bullet that had hit Hernandez had gone through his arm. Hudson had been shot twice, and despite the surgery in the Iraqi hospital, he still had a bullet buried in his back. I'm sure he had to be in pain, but he never made a sound, never let on that his wounds bothered him.

Raymond wasn't comfortable with what he was doing. I could tell that it was probably a job he wished he didn't have to do, but he did his best and wrapped the new bandages as well as he could. I wondered who these men were and why they were going out of their way to be kind.

We spent four days in the house and became comfortable with the routine. They were days of pleasant card games, conversations about going home, boredom. Sometimes the policemen gave us soda with our evening meal. We didn't hear any shooting and the walls weren't shaking from explosions.

We were able to shower and wash. I washed the one set of underwear I had, rinsing them out in the sink and laying them out near my sleep mat to dry overnight. We had been in the same set of prisoner pajamas for over two weeks and they were getting smelly and filthy, but there was nothing to change into and no way to wash the clothes.

On the fourth night, we had an excellent meal for dinner. The Major said it was hamburger, but I didn't know what it was. It sure didn't look like hamburger. Some kind of mystery meat over rice and there was plenty of it. We ate until we were full. We had soda with the meal, and when we were done, they gave us each a piece of chocolate. Chocolate! It was delicious but it made me worried. The dinner had a "last meal" feel to it, as if the next day they would take us out to shoot us. It made me nervous and I worried.

That night, I lay awake a long time, wondering what the meal meant. We had spent four days in the house, four days of them telling us we would be going home soon. Four days of hoping they were telling the truth. Were they only saying those things to make us relax, to get us feeling complacent?

The next morning, we were moved into the dining room and seated at the table. Raymond brought us our crackers and cheese with a little biscuit. The Captain brought in the tea set and I was pouring, ready to enjoy the hot brew, when I was startled by a huge bang. The walls of the house shook and I ducked instinctively.

"Get down! Get down!" I heard someone yelling. *English!* I thought. *They are yelling in English.*

We were rescued. My heart was thudding in my chest.

26

Rescue

"Get down! Get down!" they yelled as they kicked in the door. I saw Raymond immediately follow these orders. He hit the floor in a flash without hesitation and he lay unmoving, knowing the men coming in would see him as the enemy.

Marines streamed into the room in a crouching run, weapons raised and pressed to their faces. They quickly scanned the room, seeing everything at once, covering each other, ready for anything. The man in front, barely taking his face away from his weapon sight, used hand gestures to motion everyone down.

"Get down!" he yelled.

I was in shock for a moment, standing and watching what was happening, my mouth hanging open. If I hadn't known they were American, if I hadn't known they were there to rescue us, I would have been frightened by them. They looked terrifying. One Marine grabbed me by the arm and roughly pulled me to the floor. When I was down, he looked me in the eye and motioned for me to stay put. I wasn't going to argue with him.

"Okay, okay," I said. "I'll stay down."

The Captain and the Major, their hands raised, calmly joined

Raymond on the floor. Marines stood over them, checking for weapons and telling them to stay down and not to move.

A Marine grabbed me under the arm, pulled me up, and rushed me toward the door. We were leaving. We were almost free and I hesitated for a moment. I was wearing my bra, but my freshly hand-washed underwear was still slowly drying where I had left it near my sleep mat. For a second, I wanted to tell this brave Marine, who had risked everything to rescue me, to wait a minute.

My underwear, I was thinking. *I need to go get my underwear!* Somehow, sanity prevailed.

No, Shana. You're being rescued, for God's sake!

I was embarrassed but I decided to keep my mouth shut. It's hard to believe now that I even considered stopping.

The Marine who was ushering me out of the building probably wouldn't have let me go back anyway. He moved me quickly toward the door, giving me little chance to say or do anything as I hobbled along trying to keep up. Everything was happening so fast, I had little time to feel any joy. I wanted to cry but I held my tears in check. I glanced back at our captors and saw Raymond, the Captain, and the Major, prone on the floor, their fingers laced behind their heads. Marines were standing over them as if on a hair trigger to use lethal force if necessary.

"Don't hurt them," I said. "They were kind to us."

"Don't worry about it," one Marine said. "I'll take care of them."

A couple of the guys echoed what I said, but the Marines didn't hesitate in their movements. In an instant, we were outside and moving to the corner of the house.

"When I give you the signal, I want you to run over to that vehicle over there," one Marine said. He stared at me intently, letting me know we weren't out of danger yet. He pointed to an LAV (light armored vehicle) several hundred yards away.

I hadn't shed a tear yet but my self-restraint collapsed. This was exactly what I had feared.

"I can't run," I said. I was sobbing, almost losing it completely. "My legs! My legs. I can't run." I cried. I envisioned everyone getting killed because I couldn't move fast enough. I didn't want to be the cause of anyone getting hurt.

"Okay, okay," he said. "Hold on."

He draped one of my arms across his shoulders, wrapped his other arm around my waist, and carried me, his weapon in his other hand as we ran for the LAV. He moved so quickly my feet barely touched the ground. I could hear the rest of the men close behind. I didn't look around, just kept my eyes on our goal. We made it to the back of the LAV and reached the open hatch.

"Crawl up to the front," the Marine instructed.

I crawled on my hands and knees into the tiny space, moving as quickly as I could to the front, over MRE boxes and scattered equipment. Immediately the guys loaded into the LAV behind me so fast I didn't have time to sit up. I could only lie there, facedown in the back, my face in my arms. In seconds, the hatch banged shut and someone was shouting.

"Let's go! Let's go!"

And with a jolt, the vehicle started rolling.

We had been rescued. We were crying in relief. I couldn't see the men but I could hear them. We were all muttering "thank God, thank God" and sobbing in gratitude that we were finally free.

Minutes later we stopped and they unloaded us. I followed the men out of the vehicle, scrambling backward out of the open hatch, and stepped right into the arms of the first Marine I saw, bawling my eyes out in relief. I learned later his name was Staff

Sergeant Randy Meyer, the Marine who had assured me that the Major, the Captain, and Raymond would be treated fairly. For several seconds, I just buried my face in his shoulder and cried, so relieved that we were finally safe.

After a time, I wiped the tears from my face and looked around. All of us—Riley, Hernandez, Miller, Hudson, Williams, and Young—there wasn't a dry eye in the house.

A young Marine approached me, blond haired, blue eyed, so young he still had peach fuzz on his cheeks.

"United States Marine Corps, ma'am. You're going home."

A fresh wave of waterworks hit me. "You're so young," I said. "You rescued me and you're so young."

"We're just doing our job, ma'am," he said. He was grinning, though, proud of the job they had done. We all grinned. It took a few minutes for the reality to sink in. We were safe. We were free. We had been so damn lucky.

We were standing on a city street. The Marines had cordoned off the area for the rescue operation and it dawned on me that a lot of planning had gone into this. I scanned the crowd of Marines, wondering if my friend Martin was among them. I had dreamed so many nights that he would be the one to come and rescue me that the fantasy had started to feel real. Martin wasn't in the group, of course.

Someone came around to ask if anyone was injured and who needed medical attention. They gave us water and offered cigarettes to those who wanted them. I was still crying, still trying to get my head around the whole idea. It was April 13, 2003. We had been in captivity for twenty-two days.

Two Marines came over with a litter and told me to lie down so that they could carry me to the house they had set up for the rescue operation.

"Do you two realize how heavy I am?" I said.

"It's okay, ma'am. We can handle it." I wanted to walk but they insisted, so I allowed them to carry me to the house, feeling silly as I lay on the litter.

Inside the house, the Marines were enjoying their triumph, almost jumping out of their skins with joy. They were grinning and high-fiving each other, reliving the rescue and puffing out their chests at the mission they had accomplished. They had done the job without anyone getting killed or injured. There was plenty to feel happy about.

An officer came up to me, grinning from ear to ear.

"Ma'am, if you ever need anything, you just give me a call," he said. He handed me his business card. *Colonel Stacy Clardy, U.S. Marine Corps,* the card said. I thanked him and wondered how I could possible thank all of these men. They had come. They had finally come to get us.

"The men who were guarding us," I said. "What will happen to them?"

"Nothing," the colonel said. "We got a tip from someone that you were being held there. We got what we came for, so we let them go. Why do you ask?"

"They were kind to us," I said. All of the guys agreed. I hoped they would be all right.

"That woman from your unit—Private Lynch—was rescued," one of the Marines said. "Did you know?"

"Lynch is alive?!" I said. I couldn't believe it. I was so happy to hear the news. I listened to the details of her rescue and learned for the first time that Pie had died of her injuries. I knew I would be learning about everyone's fate as the days wore on.

They gave us food and sodas, and after a while, I had to use the bathroom. I asked one of the Marines where it was.

"Do you have toilet paper?" I asked him.

He looked at me a little crazy. "Sure, we have toilet paper," he said.

"YES!"

I knew I was back in the real world then. Such a small thing felt like a luxury to me. No more cotton wads, no more T-shirt strips. Real genuine toilet paper and it was wonderful.

Everyone kept asking if we needed anything, so I finally whispered to one of them what I really needed.

"Do you think I could get some underclothes?"

"What?" he said, shocked and angry. "What happened? What did they do to you?"

"Wait, calm down," I said. "You just caught me on wash day. My panties are still back at that house."

He immediately looked relieved and then attacked the new mission I had presented him with. "Okay. I think we can find something for you," he said. They got busy and found us all clean underwear and clothes if we wanted them. They rounded up some Iraqi soccer jerseys for the men. I ended up getting a pair of Colonel Clardy's underwear and a gunnery suit. The brown baggy pants and shirt didn't fit very well, but I was relieved to get out of those filthy POW pajamas. I simply couldn't spend another minute in them.

One of the Marines finally built up the courage to ask the question many of them apparently had wanted to ask.

"Can I take a picture with you?"

"Of course!" I said. And we spent several minutes having our pictures taken, together and with our Marine rescuers. It was the first of countless photos we would take with people and a small taste of what was to come.

They spent some time catching us up with current events and

said that the attack on Baghdad had only taken a few days. They told us they had been searching for us the entire time and that they knew every place we had been, learning the locations only after we were already gone. They had raided the second jail only an hour after we left, finding the dishes from our meals still sitting in our cells. They told us their intelligence sources had learned that we were to be taken to Tikrit, where Saddam and his cronies were in hiding. Evidently the plan was that we were to be used as negotiating chips in some way.

We had all talked about the feeling of the last meal we had shared in the house with Raymond, the Captain, and the Major. The ground beef and rice, the cans of soda, and the treat of dessert, the wonderful pieces of chocolate they had served. We had eaten until we were full and the meal had felt like our captors had gone out of their way to do something special for us. Maybe it was to have been our last supper with the kind Iraqi policemen without any of us being aware of it. If the Marines hadn't come during that breakfast meal, would we have been loaded back into a truck and taken to another town?

The whole time we had been in captivity, I had worried about being taken to Saddam's men, facing torture and interrogations. Saddam was the constant bogeyman, the one I feared the most. Of course, we had no idea that the brutal leader had already gone into hiding. We had guessed that the war was going our way, but there was no way to be sure. The idea that we could have been used to negotiate for Saddam's freedom or to be used as bargaining chips for him and the leaders of his brutal regime is something I don't care to think about.

The town of Samarra and the house we were in had been part of the Marine patrol area for some time. Early that morning, they had received a tip that there were POWs in the house. They hadn't even tried to get permission from higher headquarters to conduct the raid. They knew they didn't have a second to lose. As soon as they had the tip, they put together the mission and launched the raid. Major Gordon Miller, the man who pulled me down to the ground, had been in charge of the mission.

If the Marines had hesitated, taken the time to clear their operation through channels, what might have happened to us? Considering our last meal and the information that we were to be used to negotiate for Saddam and his senior leaders' freedom, these Marines may have come to get us just in the nick of time.

Of course, if things had gone badly, there would have been hell to pay for the Marines. But they had seen an opportunity and they took it, and their plan had worked perfectly. I thank God for their resolve and for Colonel Stacy Clardy's determination to execute the mission immediately. Clardy and his Marines will always be my heroes.

I looked around at the young faces of the Marines and was overwhelmed by their bravery. They had never stopped looking for us, they said. They had been looking since the day we were captured and would never have given up. They told us they had taken some losses but that the Iraqi Army was defeated and they were still searching for Saddam.

I wondered what would happen next, wondered when I could call my mother and tell her that I was okay. I wanted to hear Janelle's voice and find out what had been going on back home.

"Okay, you guys are getting out of here. The Chinooks are here for you," Colonel Clardy told us, and quickly assigned two Marines, Lance Corporal Kerney Russell and Corporal Ruben Castro, to escort us back to safety. "You are to escort them until relieved by a colonel or higher," Clardy ordered. "Until then, you stick to them."

And the two Marines did stick to us as we loaded into vehicles and were driven to a landing zone. Our Marine escort was alert and ready to go into action at any moment. We arrived at the landing zone without incident and my stomach fluttered at the sight of the huge aircraft that would take us home.

I had never ridden in a Chinook before. The massive helicopter sat quietly, the rear hatch down and waiting for us. We all shook hands with the colonel and saluted the men who had rescued us. Lance Corporal Russell helped me, and we all walked, smiling, into the belly of the massive helicopter and strapped in.

Under any other circumstances, I might have been excited about flying in a helicopter, but my mind was completely preoccupied with calling home, taking a shower, and living all of the fantasies I had played out in my head. The aircraft is too loud for conversation and the vibration was numbing. I sat in my own little world thinking about the future. I had no idea that someone had been shooting at us just after the helicopter took off. All of the guys had understood the danger we had been in. I was so preoccupied with going home that I didn't even notice.

In an hour, we landed. It took several minutes for the rotors of the helicopter to stop, making it safe for us to get off. My legs had begun to throb painfully. I had done a lot of walking and running already that day and walking was becoming more difficult. I leaned on Lance Corporal Russell as the hatch lowered and we started to disembark.

As soon as we started off the aircraft, we were surrounded by reporters. They came at us from everywhere.

27

Freedom

The Chinook took us to an airfield that was still located in Iraq, where a C-130 was waiting. We were to land directly onto the airfield and simply walk across the tarmac to board the C-130. What they hadn't planned on was the gauntlet of reporters. The mass of journalists swarmed over to us, flashes going off everywhere as they shouted questions, running, pushing, and shoving to get at us, cameras right in our faces. I heard them calling my name as if they knew me, asking me how I felt, how I had been treated.

I had told Colonel Clardy that I wanted to call my family to tell them I was okay.

"Specialist Johnson, by the time you call your family, they will have already heard about your rescue on CNN," he said.

I was shocked at how right he was. One of the Marines at the airstrip and Lance Corporal Russell were propping me up under each arm and propelling me forward, their arms out front to keep the reporters back. I was wincing in agony and trying to keep up with them as they rushed me from one aircraft to the next. Our group had become separated, the mob cutting us apart as each reporter tried to be the first to get statements from the rescued POWs.

It was a long way across the airfield from the helicopter to the plane and the reporters followed us the entire time. The first pictures of me to hit the public were of my face, screwed up in agony, the two Marines, angry and protective, helping me walk. And then there was me, clutching my raggedy old POW pajamas and my hair looking like an utter nightmare. I don't know why I wanted to keep them, maybe as some kind of a souvenir of what I had been through, but I clutched that smelly pile of clothes to my chest like a security blanket as we crossed the tarmac.

It was a relief to get away from the mob when we finally climbed aboard the plane. We filed in and were strapped into the uncomfortable webbed seats. A couple of reporters had been allowed to fly with us. I had no idea how they were selected, but they took the opportunity to take pictures and ask us how we felt. What could I say? There is only so much the word *happy* can describe.

When we finally landed in Kuwait, we were separated into groups. Those of us who had been wounded were taken to a clinic and the rest of the folks went someplace else. In no time, someone was taking my blood pressure and checking my vitals. I was waiting on a gurney for the next thing to happen when a chaplain approached me. "Do you mind if I pray with you?" he asked.

"No, sir. I don't mind at all." I had a lot to pray about, a lot to be grateful for.

The chaplain took my hand to begin the prayer, but before he could even say the first words, I started crying. I was overwhelmed with how much I had to pray about. There had been days of sheer terror, days of utter hopelessness. So many awful things that could have happened didn't. Instead there were times when I had been grateful for the kindnesses so many of our captors had shown. And now I was free and on my way home. It was overwhelming.

The chaplain saw my tears and he started crying, and in moments, everyone—the nurse, the medics, every person in the room—was crying, too. It was so moving it was funny.

"Okay, you guys gotta stop this," one of the medics said. We were laughing and crying. I was happy, just so happy to be surrounded by Americans, to be safe, to be free. We shared that prayer and it felt so good, so safe, for a change.

I was only in the clinic for a short while before someone rushed in and said I had to be on a Blackhawk to Doha, Kuwait, immediately. I thanked everyone and moved as quickly as I could to join the rest of the guys on another leg of our journey back.

The Blackhawk helicopter ride was very short. In no time we were being escorted off the aircraft and into an ambulance, then arriving at a clinic. From there it was X-rays and doctors and nurses and all kinds of people telling me where to go and what to do. I was free, but I had little freedom to do what I really wanted to do—call my family and take a shower! When I finally did get the chance to shower, they wouldn't let me take it by myself for fear that I would fall and hurt myself or something. A nursing assistant was right there, scrubbing my back and washing me. I hated it. I hated relying on other people, hated not having control of my own situation. I wanted that alone time to enjoy getting clean on my own, but they wouldn't allow it.

By the time I had finished my shower, everyone had called their families and no one had been able to get through to mine. Apparently no one was home. Where could they be? Why weren't they home waiting for my call? I could only imagine how the phone must be ringing off the hook. If it wasn't me calling, it was all the aunts and uncles calling the house after hearing about my release on the news.

Riley was talking to his family when I rejoined the group. The doctors had already told him that his sister had died while he was in captivity. She had contracted some rare neurological disease and died after having been in a coma for several days.

"Oh my God. Why did they tell you that now?" I was horrified that they would just tell him like that.

"I guess they wanted me to learn it from them before I heard it on the news," he told me. That made sense but it didn't make the news any easier to take. It dawned on me that we had a lot of news to catch up on and that a lot could have changed in the twenty-two days we were gone. What would I find when I got home?

I killed time, rolling around in the wheelchair they made me sit in, talking to the Marines and others who were standing around us, but the entire time my mind was on talking with my family, making that phone call. I was frustrated with how long it was taking to get through. They kept trying the number at my parents' house but the phone was continually busy. I could only imagine all my aunts and uncles, cousins, and friends of the family calling the house. I wanted to shout at them to get off the phone and let me get through! I tried my sister's cell phone, but Erika never answered.

We were told we would need to go through a thorough debriefing process and we were instructed not to watch any news for fear our memories would be corrupted by the way the news interpreted our story. But one of the hospital clerks went to one of the news websites where they had compiled biographies of each of us. He downloaded the bios, printed them, and gave them to us to read.

My bio had the horrible photo that had been taken as we came off the Chinook. My hair looked horrendous. It was sticking up and my face was all pinched in a painful grimace. "Oh my Lord!" I said, horrified that this was how the world would see me. It was dreadful. I wondered what else was in the news about me.

They told us we needed to go to a local Kuwaiti hospital and a long debate ensued about how we would get there. First they wanted to take us by helicopter, but Williams and Young had been shot down in helicopters and we had already ridden in a couple of choppers that day and they didn't want to fly again. Then they said we should go by convoy, but the rest of us had all been captured while riding in a convoy and we didn't want to go that way. We ended up traveling by an uneventful convoy and arrived without incident.

By the time we reached the hospital, darkness had fallen and I was getting tired. It had been a long and eventful day. A small team of people greeted us outside the hospital to ensure we got to where we needed to go. Among the group was a Kuwaiti military officer. I took one look at him, at his dark complexion, his dark hair and eyes, his thick mustache, and I was afraid of him. He looked so much like the people who had taken us prisoner. I was wheeled into the elevator and the officer, unaware of the effect his presence was having on me, stepped on with us. I was frightened to be confined in the small space with him. A nurse was pushing my gurney and I tried to cover my fear by talking to her. I started babbling about the picture on the Internet and how horrible I looked. The officer looked down at me and smiled.

"You looked beautiful in that photograph," he said.

I could feel my face heating up and I smiled, embarrassed that I had been afraid of him, and I wondered why I had been fearful.

Since it was getting late, the hospital staff had arranged rooms for us and were about to put me in a room by myself.

"No, please," I said. "Can't I be in the room with the guys?"

That request caused a bit of a stir and they discussed it for a time, but in the end, I was allowed to share a room with Miller and Young. Before I went to sleep, an orthopedic specialist examined my wounds.

"You're going to need surgery in the morning," he said. One of my wounds was becoming infected again and he wanted to go in and check out the damage.

"Okay," I said, completely unfazed by the idea of more surgery. If I could go under in a Baghdad hospital with bombs dropping and bullets flying, I could go under in Kuwait with little worry.

I was tired and in pain but I still hadn't talked to anyone back home. By this time, everyone else had spoken with their families, but mine were still either on the phone or away from it and I didn't want to go to sleep until I spoke to them. The doctor wanted to give me an injection of morphine, but they were waiting until my family could be reached.

Finally, after countless tries, I was speaking to my father.

28

Calling Home

I was so relieved to hear his voice I started crying immediately.

"Daddy!" I wailed like a little girl. He was crying in relief and telling me that everyone was there, everyone had prayed for my release, and they were overwhelmed that I was okay. I was thrilled to be talking to him. It felt real then, I was really free, and I would be going home soon. I was happy, but it was hard not to be a little pissed off at them, too. By the time my mother got on the phone, I wanted an explanation.

"Where have you been?" I asked her. "What were you doing? Everyone else spoke to their families hours ago. Where were you?" I demanded.

"Shana, we were doing something."

"Doing what?" I wanted to know. "You should have been waiting by the phone, waiting for my call."

"Oh, Shana, please don't worry about that now," she said. "We're just all so happy you're okay."

"Mom, did you see my hair?" I asked her. "Did you see how horrible it looked?"

"How can you be worrying about your hair at a time like this?"

"Well, the whole world was watching," I said. "That picture is going out all over the world, Mom. Worldwide, and I look like THAT! Hello!"

And then I asked the question that had been on my mind forever. "Can I speak to Janelle?" I asked.

"Mommy, I saw you on TV," my daughter said, and I wanted to cry.

"You did?"

"Yes. You've been gone a long time," she said.

"Yes, but I'll be home very soon, Janelle. You keep being a good girl, now, and I'll see you very soon."

We exchanged wishes of love and I spoke to my sisters and told my parents about the upcoming surgery.

Of course what my mother didn't tell me was that the entire phone conversation was being recorded for a morning television program. The entire conversation. So not only were the pictures of my horrible hair all over the world, the conversation I had with my mother about my horrible hair went out all over the world, too. The next time I talked to my mother, I let her know how I felt about that.

"I can't believe you didn't tell me it was being recorded!"

"Oh, Shana. I forgot to tell you."

"You forgot!"

It was the first taste of how life can be in the spotlight. Nothing is private. My family's phone had been ringing off the hook, not just because of my rescue, but the entire time I had been in captivity. The media called all day long looking for interviews and reactions to any tiny bit of news. My parents had received hundreds of calls a day. I had little idea of how much they had had to deal with while I was away.

As soon as I hung up the phone, the nurse pushed the morphine through my IV, and in moments, I was out for the night.

The next morning, there was some trouble while the nurses were preparing me for surgery. One of the nurses in charge of my care sounded professional as she told me what was required.

"You'll have to remove all of your jewelry," Colonel Jane Marks said. She was talking about my tongue and nipple rings. She calmly stood by while I quickly removed the ring from my tongue. I had much more trouble removing the nipple rings, however. I tried several different methods and angles but couldn't seem to get them to open. Colonel Marks tried to help but with little success. She called in another nurse, and the three of us tried everything we could think of, twisting and pulling on my nipples, but still couldn't get the damn things off.

Finally, they asked me if they could call in one of the medics.

"He has a girlfriend that wears nipple rings," Colonel Marks said. "Do you mind if we ask him to help?"

"Why not?" I said, frustrated that I couldn't get them out myself and willing to try anything to get the job done.

So they called in a young soldier who was trying his best not to look embarrassed. Soon, all three of them were pulling and twisting and tugging on my nipples trying to get the rings out. They were trying to be professional about it, but it was funny and frustrating at the same time. Finally, they were successful. Maybe I wanted to forget the embarrassment of having all of those hands all over my breasts, but it wasn't until I was on the plane to Germany that I realized that I must have left all the jewelry there in Kuwait. I haven't any idea what happened to it.

As soon as they removed the jewelry, I was taken in for surgery, which went according to plan. I woke up in my room with more pain and larger bandages. My original suspicions about my left leg were confirmed. The bullet had broken a bone on the way out and evidently had done a lot of damage. No wonder it hurt so much.

I had been walking around on a broken bone.

My one stroke of luck was in the doctor who performed the surgery. Dr. Steven Saslow was a reservist from Florida who had been ordered to active duty and sent to Kuwait in support of the war. I was told that Saslow was considered one of the best ortho-pedic surgeons in the business and he was able to repair the dam-age to my leg with just one operation.

The damage to my right leg was even worse. My Achilles tendon had been severed when the bullet traveled up my leg and exited my calf. While I wouldn't need any further surgery on the right leg, the tendon would take a long time, a very long time, to heal. I wondered how much more damage had been done to the wounds by the lack of care and my need to walk. It's amazing what you can make yourself do if you feel your life depends on it. I hoped that eventually I would at least be able to walk without pain.

Over the next several days, military intelligence people put us through intense debriefing interviews. We each took turns going into a room with a couple of folks and answered a gazillion ques-tions about what had happened to us both during the ambush of the convoy and during our captivity. The debriefings began with them giving us information about things they wanted to be sure we learned from them and not from seeing them in the press. They went over the list of killed and injured from our convoy. Most of the names we had already known, except for Sergeant Walters. He had been my supervisor, one of the noncommissioned officers in charge (NCOIC) of my section, and, as I said, he had told me that he had a feeling that he wouldn't be coming back. None of us had seen what happened to him and I had been hope-ful that he had made it, so it was hugely disappointing and sad to learn that he had died after all.

The military intelligence folks told us about the video that had been shown on all the news channels of our first minutes in the hands of our captors. They told us about Lynch's rescue and that there was video that had been shown on Arab TV that displayed the bodies of the soldiers from our unit who had been killed in the ambush. The video was on several Internet sites. They wanted us to know what had been happening in the news so that we wouldn't be shocked by it.

After that, it was hours and hours of questions. We spent three days under questioning in Kuwait and the debriefings continued once we arrived in Germany as well. Since I couldn't be moved after my surgery, they weren't letting us leave the hospital anyway, so we spent the time getting debriefed.

I called home every day. The first thing I wanted to do was to reassure my family that I hadn't been raped. I knew they wanted to ask, so I wanted to take the worry away for them. After we covered those topics, I would give them a rundown of what was on tap for us that day, how things were progressing. They kept asking when I was going to be home and I didn't have an answer for them. I knew we were going to Germany for a stay at the hospital in Landstuhl, but I didn't know how long we would have to be there. We had appointments with intelligence debriefers, with psychiatrists and medical doctors. And it wouldn't be the Army if there wasn't a mountain of paperwork to complete.

One positive thing that resulted from the embarrassing phone conversation that had aired on the morning news program was that someone from Camp Doha came to the hospital to do my hair. This woman took my braids out and washed what felt like mounds of sand out of my hair. She conditioned it and relaxed it and styled it. It felt so good to have my hair finally done, to have it finally looking decent again. It did wonders for my spirits.

When we weren't seeing doctors or being interviewed, we

watched movies, talked, and relaxed. I had stacks of mail to go through. I was given a package my mother had sent to me long before we left on the convoy and inside was something that went a long way toward making me feel normal again. Underwear. My mother had sent me underwear!

After three days in the hospital in Kuwait, we were on our way to Germany. They gave each of us a black backpack because now we had stuff to carry, things we needed to take with us. I still had that set of POW pajamas and that was one thing I put in my backpack. They had issued us a full set of uniforms, desert camouflage jackets, pants and T-shirts, boots, socks, and caps. We wore the uniforms on our trip to Germany, which was another step closer to getting us all home.

We boarded a C-141, a large cargo plane that was filled with wounded on their way to Germany and the large Army hospital there. The wounded, some of them seriously, were on litters attached to the sides of the aircraft stacked five or six high. Some of them had heart monitors; most had some kind of IV attached to them. Some were almost completely covered in bandages; many were amputees. Doctors and nurses moved among the wounded, checking on them, giving medications. It was hard to look at all of those young people so horribly maimed. I was strapped to a litter, but my wounds were minor compared to what some of them were facing.

At one point, I had to use the bathroom and was offered a bedpan, but I refused it. I could walk to the bathroom, I insisted, and set out to get there on my own. I climbed down from my litter, and since I couldn't put weight on my right leg, I hopped down the aisle. Soldiers and Marines held their hands out as support, steadying me, helping me along, propping me from one to the next until I made it to the bathroom. They were bandaged and maimed and they reached out to help me.

"It's great to see you," some of them said.

"So glad you're free," they said.

They lay there bloody and wounded and they had words of encouragement for me. It was amazing.

The flight was agonizingly long. We hit bad weather patches and had to go around, but eventually we landed at the airstrip. We taxied, then stopped, and it seemed like we waited a long time. Finally someone came around and gathered up the seven of us. There was such a huge media mob on the airfield that they needed to take us off the airplane first before they could unload the rest of the wounded. It angered me. I looked around at all the brave men and women who had been so seriously wounded and I couldn't believe the media would overlook them to get to us. It was frustrating but there was nothing we could do.

They asked us to please wave at the media so that they would be satisfied, so I waved and gave the victory sign as my gurney was rolled across the tarmac. I couldn't believe the wall of flashes, the horde of press that was there to get shots of us.

By this time it was late at night and I was feeling worn out from the flight, but there was no way any of us were getting to sleep. There was a TV in our room, and I turned it on and immediately saw myself getting wheeled across the tarmac to the ambulance. It was odd to sit there and watch myself, see the pictures that had been dredged up from my past flash across the screen and listen to strangers talk about my condition.

"It is not known if she will need additional surgery," one news report said. I looked at the doctor who was in the room and asked, "Will I need more surgery?" We laughed at how odd the situation was.

Our short walk from the aircraft to the hospital was replayed over and over and it obviously wasn't enough. The media were hounding the hospital for more, so the Army public affairs people asked us to go out on the balcony the next day and talk to them. We instantly agreed that Chief Williams would be our spokesperson. We planned to stand there as a group as he answered questions.

In the morning Sergeant First Class Stewart came to braid my hair for the occasion. The process took hours, so she worked on my head while we were given briefings by Army legal folks who told us what paperwork we would have to complete to get reimbursed for all of the things we lost in the ambush. I had no idea that I could get a kind of insurance payment for the duffel bags full of my clothing and gear that had been stolen or destroyed. The briefings and paperwork seemed endless, and the soldier kept braiding my hair the entire time.

"Do you think I should stop?" she asked me at one point.

"No," I said. "They can watch and learn a little something about what it takes to care for hair like mine."

Besides, I was determined that the next time the press saw me, my hair would be in a presentable state for a change.

A local three-star general had come to the hospital to visit us just before we went out for our balcony appearance. He watched with us as we turned the TV on and saw that all the channels were showing a shot of the empty balcony and they talked about how they were waiting for us to come out. I was surprised when the general grabbed the handles and pushed my wheelchair outside. We emerged onto the balcony and were greeted by a wall of photographers and video cameras. We just stood there for a few minutes and waved, the whir and electronic click of cameras going off all around us. Dave said a few words and we all waved. Before I was wheeled off the balcony, I looked at the cameras and waved. "Hi, Mom. Hi, Dad," I said. I couldn't resist.

29

Good Wishes

A couple of us needed some things from the little convenience store in the hospital. Wounded soldiers are evacuated so quickly from Iraq and Afghanistan that they arrive at Landstuhl Regional Medical Center in Germany without any possessions. They, like the seven of us were, are given basic supplies to tide them over—clothing, shoes, and a calling card from charity organizations like the USO (United Services Organization) and the Red Cross. Army Emergency Relief (AER) gives each wounded soldier a check for a hundred dollars to buy things like toothpaste and soap.

So with our hundred-dollar checks in hand, we wandered down to the convenience store with thoughts of buying thank-you cards for all the people who had helped us or to pick up a thing or two. A short shopping trip to browse and see what was there. It seemed like a simple idea at the time, but it wasn't. We were mobbed. We had been warned. We were told that people would react to seeing us, and even after the whole balcony news appearance with the scores of cameras, I still wasn't prepared for how people swarmed around us wanting to get a firsthand look.

Suddenly visitors to the hospital were asking for autographs, asking if they could have their picture taken with me. I exchanged looks of disbelief with the guys. Everyone was saying they were happy we made it home safely, that they were happy to see us, but they were surrounding us and there was no graceful exit save for smiling and agreeing to the requests. It was my first exposure to the demands this new recognition was going to bring. It was a little scary to have so many people coming at us at once. I kept smiling and tried to be nice, but I didn't understand what people expected from me or how I was supposed to react. It felt like I was being treated like I was some kind of celebrity and I am so not that!

Most of the time it was heartwarming to know that so many people had worried about us. It was heartwarming to us, but the hospital was inundated with calls and with people coming by to see us. Because there were so many, the hospital refused everyone. Some friends I had been stationed with at Fort Carson had stopped by but were forced to just leave cards with good wishes. Even my cousin Andre, who was stationed in the area, had been turned away.

When I learned that Andre had been sent home, I threw a little fit. I wanted to see some family. The hospital tracked him down and he came back, bringing his wife and daughters with him. It had been years since I had seen the big strapping staff sergeant. He had been a playmate when we were kids and now here he was, outranking me. I hardly recognized the man he had become. We spent time talking about my experience and I introduced him proudly to the guys. Andre told me that he was shipping out to Iraq in just a couple of weeks. I was surprised at how much this news bothered me. I showed him my wounds and talked about the disastrous convoy, but it didn't seem to deter him. He was ready to do his duty and go where he was ordered.

One day while we were still being treated at Landstuhl, two of the Marines who had been on the mission to rescue us stopped by to say hello. They were tentative and shy when they approached us in a hallway. They looked tired and worn down, as if they still had some of the troubles of the desert on their faces, but they were happy to see us and wished us all luck in our recovery.

After all of the happy talk, they told us that directly after our rescue, the unit of Marines had continued on their mission. Just a few hours after making sure we were on our way back home, they had been ambushed. The two young men we were talking with had been injured in the attack. One of the guys in their unit, a Marine who had helped to save my life, had been killed.

I remembered how ecstatic they had all been at the success of their mission, all the high fives and smiles and cheers of triumph they had displayed directly after our rescue. They had all been so full of life only to be plunged into such danger so quickly after. Despite the danger, the two young Marines wanted to recover as quickly as possible so they could rejoin their unit and return to the fight.

On our last night in Germany, some of the officers in charge of us took us out to a restaurant in an old castle. It was a wonderful evening. The weather was fine. We were all cleaned up and wearing civilian clothes and feeling like normal people again. It was my first time out in the real world, away from uniforms and hospitals. We sat down to a civilized meal and I finally, finally had that thick steak, with the steaming baked potato, and despite being on pain medications, I had my tall, cold glass of beer.

The next day, we flew home. I was still on pain medications and slept most of the way. When we finally landed at Fort Bliss, Williams and Young were rushed off to get on another plane headed for Fort Hood, Texas, where they were stationed. The rest of us didn't even get a chance to say good-bye to them. There were so many screaming people around and so much going on that the two pilots were simply taken away without our knowing it. Later, when everything died down and we realized what had happened, the five of us got pretty upset about the way their departure was handled. The folks in charge obviously didn't understand that we needed that closure, the chance to say a proper good-bye to the two men who had been so crucial in making sure we got home safely.

But at the time, when we first landed, we had no idea that Williams and Young had already left.

We were greeted by over three thousand people, most of them holding signs and waving flags. Only immediate family was allowed to approach us after we got off the plane. My parents, sisters, and daughter rushed forward and surrounded my gurney. There were buckets of tears and lots of hugs. It was so good to see them all. Janelle was scared by all of the excitement, the big crowd, and all of the cameras, but I assured her everything was okay. It was hard to believe that I was finally hugging her.

Hudson, Riley, Miller, Hernandez, and I climbed into a golf cart and rode in front of the crowd waving and smiling. My dad brought an American and a Panamanian flag for me to wave and I smiled, waved, and displayed both flags. We stopped at one point, and since Williams wasn't there to be spokesman anymore, Riley was forced into the role. He got out of the golf cart and said a few words to the crowd. He talked about how good it was to be back in America and thanked everyone for all of their good wishes. We climbed back into the cart and rode around for a bit, giving the crowd what they had come for. My entire brood, it seemed, had come to the airfield for the occasion—aunts, uncles, and cousins. Even my eighty-year-old grandmother in her wheelchair was there.

Me and the guys along with our families finally left the huge crowd and were taken into the deployment center. I was surprised when I was told that Army authorities wanted me to go to the William Beaumont Army Medical Center in El Paso for further tests and checkups. I just wanted to go home.

"No way," I said. "I am not going to another hospital."

"Someone needs to administer your pain medications," the doctor said.

"My aunt is a registered nurse," I told him. "She's been to the Gulf War, she knows how to care for the wounded, and she's right outside. She can make sure I'm okay."

"There are more tests we need to do," he said.

"I can come back for those. I just want to go home!"

"Your dressings need changing," he said.

"She's a registered nurse, for God's sake," I insisted. "She will take care of everything, believe me."

I had never argued with an officer like that before. I was at the end of my rope and there was no way I was going back to a damn hospital bed. They finally sent a soldier out to get my aunt. She came in and the doctors briefed her on my wounds and what medication I was taking. She looked down at me and then looked at those doctors.

"I have the situation under control," my aunt Maggie said.

I was so relieved. We were finally released, finally able to leave, but I still wasn't able to go home. Since our rescue, the already overwhelming media gaggle at our house had become a regular mob scene. Our house had been surrounded by reporters for days and the phone was ringing off the hook. On the day of my arrival, Army force protection folks knew it would be difficult to even get near the house, let alone ensure that everyone would be safe, so they had arranged for rooms for us at the distinguished visitors' quarters. It wasn't home but at least I was surrounded by family. We were scattered around four large rooms and we settled in for several days.

I shared a room with my aunt Maggie. She cared for me and made sure I took my medications. I wasn't the easiest patient. I was irritable and cranky. There were times when I lashed out and she was the one who bore the brunt of my frustrations.

No matter how horrible I was, she still pushed my wheelchair and went with me to my appointments. Everywhere we went on Fort Bliss caused a stir, so when I had appointments at the hospital, which was almost every day, the staff devised a policy to make sure I was seen by the doctors first to get me out of the way. I objected to that special treatment. There were a lot of people far sicker than me who were forced to wait until I was seen.

"They want to get you taken care of so people don't stand around and gawk," Aunt Maggie said.

"It's not fair," I argued. "They were here first."

"But the longer you're here, the harder it is for the staff to do their job."

"I just don't like it!" I was almost yelling at her and none of it was her fault. She tried to hide her tears, but I could see that I had made her cry, and that was just one in a list of times when I took my frustration out on my aunt. I was horrible, but she was there for me. She double-checked every test result, making sure the results were interpreted correctly and that I wasn't going through unnecessary procedures. She was a saint. I still feel horrible about the way I treated her.

There were times when I simply lost it. Being back home with my family around and having so many people sending me things, wishing me well, showing such support, was overwhelming. I couldn't get over the guilt I felt. Why were people treating me like

I was some kind of hero? I wasn't brave. I had merely survived when others didn't. It was confusing and overwhelming, and as much as I tried to fake it, I wasn't dealing with it very well.

Strangers sent me gifts, cards, letters, even money. They sent stacks of stuffed animals; one man made me a beautifully carved cane, a one-of-a-kind, hand-whittled walking stick. It was beautiful and unique. People sent me handmade quilts and blankets, some with my name sewn into them. I looked at those handmade gifts and was flabbergasted by the hours that had gone into making them and couldn't understand why they were sent to me. I didn't understand why I was being rewarded for living when eleven of us had died. Those first days were just a hint of how I would feel as time wore on.

I had boxes of letters and cards to sort through. A lot of people sent me money and I had to send it back. I tried to write notes to explain why I wasn't allowed to accept the money, to thank them and suggest they send the money to the Red Cross or Army Emergency Relief. It was weeks and weeks before I could sort through it all. There were so many people I wanted to write back to and it took me a long time, but I eventually returned notes to the ones to whom I could.

One woman sent me a beautiful leather-bound Bible with my name engraved in gold letters on the cover. A legal adviser on the base said I had to send it back to her because it had a value over the legally acceptable gift-giving amount. It was so beautiful, though, and I could tell such thought had gone into the gift that I didn't want to part with it. I called a judge advocate general's office in the Pentagon and talked to the military's version of a lawyer. I explained the details about the Bible, and after hearing that it had been engraved with my name, the military lawyer said that I could keep it.

That was a relief. I hated to send such a thoughtful gift back and it bothered me that the local JAG had so offhandedly told me to reject it. The more I dealt with the local JAG office, the more I started to gather hints about how some of the people at Fort Bliss were beginning to feel about our presence and the stir our rescue had caused. We were causing them a lot of extra work, from the hospital to the JAG office and the local public affairs office, the people who had to deal with the hordes of press who wanted to talk to us. I knew we were causing all of them headaches, but none of us had asked for any of this, not the attention from the public, not our wounds, and certainly not the hordes of media folks.

The days in the guesthouse surrounded by my family were a constant flow of people and activities. They drove me crazy with taking pictures. When Riley came in one day to talk to me, my cousins grabbed a camera and started snapping pictures of us together. They would hug the guys and talk to them and it was always a little embarrassing for me. The people in my family are all a little crazy, and when you get them all together in one place, there's no telling what any of them might say or do.

Eventually they all got around to telling me what it was like to learn about my capture. My father told me that he had been channel-surfing, looking for a cartoon for Janelle to watch. He flipped to Telemundo, the Spanish-language channel that broadcasts in the United States, and saw a news headline that said something about an attack on an American convoy.

My father, having been a senior noncommissioned officer, and having a daughter he knew to be a part of the mission, stopped and listened to every word. The news in Spanish said the 507th Maintenance Company had been ambushed, that several unit members had been killed and several taken prisoner, including a black female.

My dad knew I wasn't the only black female in the 507th, but the little information he received from that initial report was enough for him to start to worry. As soon as my mother came home from church, he told her what he had heard. They discussed it for a while and reassured each other that it wasn't me before my mother left for work. What were the odds, after all? It had to be some other black female in the 507th Maintenance Company, not their Shana!

My mother left for work but couldn't keep the news out of her head. As soon as she had a spare moment, she called one of her sisters, in near hysterics.

"It's Shana," my mother wailed. "I know it's her!"

But my aunt Sonja calmly assured my mother that it couldn't be me. What were the odds? It had to be someone else. My mother, after much coaxing, finally calmed down and, agreeing that the odds were too great and that her daughter was probably just fine, hung up, at least pretending that she had been convinced of the impossibility of my having been captured by the enemy.

Of course, as soon as Aunt Sonja hung up the phone with my mother, she immediately called another aunt, in near hysterics, crying that I had been captured and was now probably being tortured by the Iraqi military.

This pattern went on and on until every aunt had tearfully reassured another that what they all knew to be true was actually false and that they shouldn't worry because *of course* Shana was just fine.

When my sister Erika told me this story, I laughed and laughed. We all laughed. I could so picture the mad dialing of one aunt to the next, the calm words of wisdom they bestowed to reassure the panic of their sister, then their immediate need to pass on the awful information to the next one.

Then, like the rest of the world, they all saw the horrible video that played over and over on CNN. They saw my eyes darting back and forth between the man speaking Arabic and the English translator. They saw how rigid I was, not realizing that I was in debilitating pain or that I was suffering from shock, and they all came to the stark realization that I was in extreme danger. I can't even imagine how it must have felt for them to see that video for the first time. I can only imagine how I would have reacted had it been one of my sisters instead of me.

When my family saw the proof of my capture, they were all in hysterics again, and who could blame them? Eventually, they would settle into a pattern of prayer and mutual reassurance. For every day that I was in custody, they were in their own kind of prison. I sometimes think I had it easier, since I knew what I was facing, knew the realities of my situation. My family, on the other hand, had only their imaginations to rely on, and that left a wide range of horrific possibilities for them to envision.

Daily, I went to the hospital for tests and examinations while the rest of the brood were wined and dined by the city of El Paso or other groups that offered them lunches and tours. They were having a great time, and since I love them all to death, it was okay that they got on my nerves a little bit.

Janelle was having a hard time with things. My legs, wrapped tightly in bandages, frightened her. She refused to come near me. It broke my heart. I would talk to her and try to reassure her that it was okay, but she would hide behind things, stare at me, cry, and refuse to budge. She would stand across the room and just call to me.

"Mommy?" she would say.

"Yes, I'm right here." She would stare at me from a distance as if trying to connect the familiar voice with the person with the scary bandages she was seeing.

After one set of surgeries, my right leg was encased in a kind of large boot. Janelle was especially afraid of the boot. It was more than a week at my parents' house before she finally decided that it was okay. Aunt Maggie spent a lot of time working on her, reassuring her. Aunt Maggie would tell her to come closer and touch my legs, telling her they were nothing to be afraid of. Finally, after many days, Janelle felt comfortable enough to actually put the boot on and clomp around in it.

My aunt Maggie noticed, even before I did, that I might be suffering from PTSD (post-traumatic stress disorder). She mentioned it to me a number of times, then finally blew up at one of my doctors.

"Look at her," she said. "She acting differently, she's losing her temper inappropriately, she's irritable, what more evidence do you need? You're a doctor, for God's sake. Do your job!"

I was shocked to hear her say such a thing. We had been warned before we left Landstuhl about all the signs. I listened to the doctors and their warnings, hearing them but knowing inside there was no reason to worry. I figured I was able to handle anything my freedom threw at me. I was going home! It was going to be great and wonderful and everything I had imagined. I was going to be free.

So when my aunt told the doctors that she thought I needed psychiatric help, I was appalled. I wanted to tell her she was wrong, that everything was okay and I could handle whatever happened. But as much as I didn't want to admit it, she was right. I was depressed. I would cry at times for minor reasons. Most times I had no idea what had triggered the response; I would just suddenly be crying. I would snap at people for no reason, and unfortunately, my aunt Maggie was usually the most convenient person on which to vent my frustrations. The worst part was that I felt such grinding guilt about surviving that I often thought I should correct what luck had dealt me and kill myself.

One day, my parents told me something my daughter had asked them.

"Why is Mommy crying all the time?" she asked.

I was shocked and saddened and couldn't help the feeling of guilt that swept over me. Hearing about her innocent question finally made me realize how confused she must be and how much my emotional swings were affecting her. It was the event that finally made me acknowledge that I had a serious problem that I wasn't going to be able to fix by myself. I had been raised to be a strong, independent woman, and despite the turmoil I had been through, I thought I should be able to just shake it off and drive on, but after hearing the painful question from my daughter, I finally had to admit that I needed psychiatric help.

Admitting the problem was a major step, but still, only the first step in a very long road I needed to travel.

30

Hoopla

We started getting invitations to a lot of huge events, events that, in my life before becoming a POW, I never would have dreamed of attending. Some were impossible to turn down. Lonestar invited us to attend the Country Music Awards in Las Vegas. Miller brought his wife, I brought my little sister, and Young brought his new girlfriend, Kelly, who was Miss South Carolina.

Ron and Kelly met after Ron got home and the two of them had just started dating at the time of the awards event. Unlike me, Ron's new girlfriend seemed very comfortable with the idea of having celebrity status. I guess it's all part of being a beauty queen. In fact, she was so comfortable with the spotlight that a couple years later, Ron and Kelly ended up going on *The Amazing Race* together.

The invitation to go to the awards show came to us through official Army channels, so we wore our uniforms and were asked to get up onstage for a special tribute. I was nervous about the whole thing, but I shouldn't have been. Everyone was very nice to us, going out of their way to make us feel comfortable. We waited in the front row for our part of the program. Then we did our bit in front of the huge audience and the cameras. When it was over, we went back to our front-row seats. I sat between Lee Ann Womack and Wynonna Judd, who were both very nice. Never in a million years would I have predicted attending an awards show like that. We went to the after party and met more celebrities than I could name.

I did a big round of talk shows, from *Ellen* to *Oprah*. I had the most fun going on the Jay Leno show. They flew me and Janelle and Erika out to Los Angeles and put us up in a fancy hotel. On the day of the show, Jay came into the the green room, where we were waiting for my turn to go on. He sat on the floor with Janelle and gave her a gift and watched her open it. It was a little pink dinosaur and it was sweet of him to sit there for a few minutes and pay genuine attention to my daughter. Maybe his show was my favorite because it was my first. I just remember that he was kind and friendly and understood how nervous I would be. He told me to be myself and I was. It was simple but good advice and I have always remembered it.

I was given ringside seats to an Oscar De La Hoya fight in Vegas. The invitation included the trip to Vegas, a fancy suite of rooms at the hotel, and star treatment at the fight. It was red-carpet treatment all the way. While I was in Vegas, the mayor even gave me the key to the city.

Jessica and I were invited to be in *Glamour* magazine's Women of the Year issue. We both had big *Glamour* photo shoots a couple of months before the awards event. Then, at the show in New York, Jessica and I posed for pictures for the paparazzi. It was the first time the two of us had been photographed together and the press went totally insane. Even the people at *Glamour* commented that they had never seen anything like the photo frenzy that went on over us. Britney Spears was there, and even she was getting less attention than we were. It was madness.

"This is crazy," I said.

"This is show business," one of the photographers said.

I was still in the Army at the time, so whenever I went on an official event like that, I wore my uniform. But once the official event was over, *Glamour* did my hair and makeup and dressed me with a great outfit for the after party.

I'll always remember the invite to drop the ball in Times Square on New Year's Eve. Mayor Michael Bloomberg invited me and a bunch of my family. My parents and sisters, my daughter, and my nieces were all invited and we were joined by many aunts and uncles. The star treatment started with a fancy town car ride to the airport in El Paso. We were met at the airport in New York and whisked off to a beautiful hotel in the city. December 31, 2003, was a hectic day. I didn't sleep well the night before since there was so much scheduled and it was all a little overwhelming. The day began on Wall Street, where I was invited to ring the opening bell on the New York Stock Exchange. Directly after that, I did an interview on *The Early Show*. There was lunch and dinners, tours of the city, and then it was time to get ready for that wild party in Times Square. I was nervous about having to hit the button that would make the ball drop.

"What happens if I screw it up?" I asked. I was afraid I would ruin the New Year's Eve celebrations, not just for all the people in Times Square, but for all those millions who were watching on TV.

"Don't worry," they told me. "It's really automatic. The ball will drop at the right time no matter what you do."

That made me feel a lot better, but it was still nerve-racking waiting for my turn to flip that big switch. Of course everything went off without a hitch and my entire family got to party down.

The public affairs office on base handled most of the requests for our appearances. I was still a soldier and any request that came in had to be approved by my superiors and permission granted from the Army higher-ups. I know the office was short-staffed and wasn't really prepared to handle the volume of calls and requests that came in and it started to become clear that they wanted things to slow down. I found out after the fact that *People* magazine had wanted to include me in their Person of the Year issue. I would have been one of many people recognized in the issue, but the PAO office sat on the request and never let me know about it until the magazine was already on the newsstands. I was disappointed to have missed the opportunity and a little worried about what other things I might have missed out on just because someone decided not to pass the word along to me.

Despite the magazine issue, it is still amazing how many different things we were invited to do and even more amazing how much of it I barely remember. My first few weeks back home, I was medicated for pain and it seems like I went through some events in kind of a daze. I wanted to accept any invitation I received while I was on convalescent leave because being at Fort Bliss, being around the soldiers in my unit who hadn't been through what I had been through, feeling guilty to be alive, and feeling the bitterness from others in the unit was too much. The invitations were a way to get away from all of that.

My father kept after me to keep track of all of the invitations somehow, to catalog the gifts and awards, to make a list of everything that happened so that I wouldn't forget. I did keep track of some things, but if you asked me today to list them all, I probably couldn't do it.

The only real souvenir I kept of my captivity were the POW pajamas I had been wearing when we were rescued. I tried to throw the smelly things away, but a nurse in Doha told me to keep them, insisting that I would want to have them one day. I folded the smelly things up and put them in the black backpack I'd been given. I gave them to my dad and he still has them. He is a big keeper of things, insisting that Janelle will want to know all the details as she gets older.

"Your daughter is going to want to know what these days were like," my dad says. I know he's right and I do try to keep better track of things now, but those first few weeks and months are still very much a blur.

One thing I do remember very clearly is all of the talk about making money. My parents had been approached by producers and publishers while I was still in captivity, all vying for the rights to my story. They had suffered the endless phone calls and strangers knocking on their door trying to get to them to make money, money, money. Naturally, when I got back, my parents wanted to talk to me about book deals and movie deals. They were tentative in their approach, not sure how I would react to the talk of profiting from what had happened to me. They explained the deals, making it sound easy, like a natural thing for me to do. At the time, I simply couldn't handle the idea of doing anything like that.

"Shana, it could secure a future for you and Janelle," my father said.

"No," I said. "I'm not ready for all of that."

They would immediately back off, but sometime later, they would bring it up again. I had been lucky. I had survived and I was happy about that, but I just couldn't see using the experience to make a bunch of money. But money was on a lot of people's minds. I don't know how many conversations I had about money.

As much fun as I was having, a lot of people, besides the overworked public affairs office, weren't happy about all of the attention we ex-POWs were getting, and soon enough their attitudes became a problem I could no longer ignore.

31

No Hero

My wounds were much worse than I had originally thought. Recovery was slow and it was evident my legs would never be the same. The slow recovery meant that coming home was much harder than I had imagined. I was still a soldier, and even if I was on convalescent leave, I still had the responsibilities of a soldier. I had expected that the Army would be my life, the way it had been my father's life and the way so many of my aunts and uncles had made the military their lives. I knew that to stay in the Army, I'd have to face some serious physical challenges, but I was prepared to try. What I wasn't prepared for was all the resentment and pettiness that made it nearly impossible to continue a life in uniform.

I was still the same Shana who had worked in the kitchen at the DFAC, the same person who had cooked meals and served them to several hundred people on base, but suddenly my nail polish was too bright. My boots weren't shiny enough. There was some invisible infraction that involved my uniform or there was some other thing I was doing wrong.

Not too long after I came off convalescent leave, a senior

noncommissioned officer accused me of fraud, claiming that I had been falsely receiving benefits for family housing when I should have been living in single-soldier quarters. This NCO claimed that my daughter had always lived with my parents and not with me. If Janelle had been in the custody of my parents, I would have been required to live in a single-soldier barracks. Since she lived with me, I had the benefit of family housing on base. Of course, Janelle was only with her grandparents during my deployment and during my convalescence, but the soldier had made serious allegations of fraud, which could have cost me thousands of dollars, loss of rank, and even jail time. The accusations were groundless but it still took an investigation and the involvement of the post commander and the senior-ranking noncommissioned officer, the command sergeant major, on base to get things cleared up.

I can't speculate about what motivated this person to bring the charges against me. I didn't know the man, so there wasn't any way for me to really know why he did it. What I do know is that being accused of attempted fraud of the federal government is a serious thing. When people hear that you're being investigated, they look at you differently. I was innocent, but my reputation had been disparaged nonetheless.

The whole experience was hurtful and is still hard for me to understand.

No matter how I might have felt about things, I was being treated differently than most other soldiers. Each day I put on my uniform, and on the days when morning formation was held, I stood in the ranks like everyone else to report my readiness for duty to the first sergeant. A first sergeant is like the supervisor of the operation. He knows what tasks management expects to be completed each day and he keeps track of where everyone is and what they are doing. When it came to me and the other POWs, our first sergeant had his hands full.

I was on light duty, which wasn't unusual. Soldiers get hurt and it's not unusual for someone to have a physical profile that excludes them from engaging in physical training or doing their normal job. But we weren't just on profile. We were also engaged in an almost daily calendar of public appearances and media events. While I was in uniform, the events I was sent to weren't all of my choosing. I was ordered to attend and participate in many of the appearances by the Army. Army public affairs was involved with getting my face out there for the world to see and that meant leaving Fort Bliss and the control of my unit command whether they liked it or not. My first sergeant was very supportive of me and helped with arrangements to ensure I got to the places I was supposed to be, but it became clear that there was growing dissatisfaction from our battalion command. They were growing weary of my duties away from the unit and they were giving the first sergeant a hard time about it.

If I was sent to participate in an event that took place off the installation or that involved an overnight stay, someone had to generate a set of military orders for me. Travel and hotel costs of most events that involved a civilian organization, like appearing on the Jay Leno show, were paid for by the organization, but I still had to have orders, and the logistics of who would pay for what always had to be discussed and worked out through the military bureaucracy.

All of this meant a lot more work for the folks in our administration office, more work for the commander to approve and sign off on, and more work for my first sergeant, since if I was on military orders to appear somewhere, he had to make sure I got there as ordered. The celebrity status of us ex-POWs became a headache for the command and I'm sure they were all wondering just how long they would have to put up with it. And there's no denying that much of what they were sending me to was pretty darn cool. I was being sent to these exciting places like the Jay Leno show and some people in the unit were left to figure out the logistics. It wasn't long before the resentment began to build.

The one thing senior leadership could control was the way I looked in my uniform. Senior NCOs and officers from the battalion passed complaints down to my first sergeant, correcting any minor infraction they saw or thought they saw. If my nail polish was not muted enough for someone in uniform, they complained to him about it. If my medals weren't aligned exactly right on my dress uniform, someone had something to say about it. That's just the way it was.

I tried to not pay too much attention to the attitude, though, and each day, when everyone else went to a job, I went about the various appointments that had been arranged for that day. I usually had some kind of physical therapy or other medical appointment. I also reported to the public affairs office to go through the mail that had come in and to discuss the invitations for public appearances or media events.

One day a soldier in my battalion approached me, angry that I had been sent to Las Vegas to see the De La Hoya fight.

"Why do you get to go to the fight?" he asked, angry and accusatory. "I was in Iraq. I'm a veteran. How come I don't get to go to those things?"

I didn't want to get into an argument with him about it. After all, I wasn't feeling like I was someone special who should be given special treatment either, but the invitations were coming, and in many cases, the Army wanted us to represent the military at the events. Sometimes, I didn't have much of a choice. As time went on, the jealousy and pettiness grew more and more unavoidable.

Many of the events or appearances happened right on Fort Bliss. For the first year, we were invited to ceremonies and events that were taking place around the installation, treated as VIPs, and used basically as a media draw. If one of the POWs from the 507th was going to be there, the press would be there. The public affairs office and others in charge took advantage of that often and invited us to change-of-command ceremonies, Veterans Day and Memorial Day events—any time an event was going on, Miller, Reilly, Hernandez, Hudson, and I would be invited.

I was a specialist at the time but still a junior-ranking soldier, not of the rank of someone who would normally hobnob with officers' wives, field-grade officers, or generals, for that matter. Despite my lowly rank, I was seated in the VIP sections during ceremonies and invited to the receptions that took place after the ceremonies, receptions that were for invited guests only. People wanted to meet me and I was made available to them, dressed up in my green uniform jacket and pants with all of my medals and putting my best face on for the situation.

Almost six months after my release, I attended one such event on Fort Bliss. I was talking to the garrison commanding general's wife, a very nice woman who always had a kind word for me and went out of her way to make me feel comfortable at the sometimes very stuffy affairs. The two of us were sharing a laugh about something when I saw a colonel pull the garrison command sergeant major aside. The colonel pointed at me as he said something to the sergeant major and he didn't look too happy.

Later, I asked the sergeant major what the colonel had said and was told that he was questioning what a junior enlisted soldier was doing at the event and the sergeant major had to explain who

I was. It was clear to me from observing the colonel that the sergeant major's explanation of who I was hadn't appeased him. The colonel, whoever he was, didn't think it appropriate for me to be there.

As soon as I was back from Iraq my father had suggested I consider getting out of the Army. Part of me suspects that he didn't want to live with the idea of my ever having to go back to a war zone. What he told me was that he believed the resentment would continue to grow.

"Those officers and senior NCOs who are supporting you now will move on or retire and they won't be there to stand up for you. The situation is going to get worse before it gets better."

My father was right, of course. We were released from captivity in April 2003, and by late August of that year, I had spoken to the commander of the hospital to request a medical discharge. The doctors and nurses tried to talk me into staying and made me wait several weeks before they began the paperwork process. Once the process was started, I knew I had made the right decision. I simply couldn't stay in the Army any longer.

The negative opinions I was getting from people weren't just about our public appearances or our celebrity status. It wasn't long before it became clear that people in the unit and others whom I encountered blamed us, the ones who had been ambushed, for what had happened to us. They claimed our weapons were dirty and poorly maintained and that it was our fault so many of them had malfunctioned. Of course, none of them knew about the sticky tape we had been ordered to put on our magazines or that we had spent far longer, forty-eight hours longer, tooling through the open desert, hours in which our weapons collected more dirt and dust with no time for stopping or cleaning them, not to mention no rest.

They said we were stupid to have gotten lost and stupid to have wandered into the middle of a city and that we deserved to have been ambushed for our stupidity. Of course they didn't know about the radios we couldn't get repaired or about our inability to communicate with our higher headquarters, or that the TCP had left us as if we had been completely forgotten and that no one came back to check on us. In reality, any one of the people who had criticized us for our performance could have been lost under the same circumstances. Sure, we had been lost, but our higher headquarters shared responsibility for that. They should have known we were out there. They should have made sure we were on the right track. They should have come back for us.

The thing that really pissed me off was that so many of them thought we had just gotten our asses kicked and didn't fight back. They didn't know about Miller, the young soldier who had fought so bravely. They didn't know about Sergeant Walters, who had died fighting the enemy to the end despite being wounded multiple times, or about all the others in the unit, Chief Mata and Private Sloan, who fought bravely until they were killed in action. Or about Specialist James Grub, Staff Sergeant Traik Jackson, or Sergeant Curtis Campbell, all of whom had been wounded multiple times and helped to save others in their unit by continuing to fight despite their injuries until they could finally rally and get away. And they never acknowledged the others in the unit who had fought their way out of that mess, the ones like Sergeant Mathew Rose who had fought and survived despite impossible odds. They didn't take into account how surrounded we had been or how outnumbered we were or that we were support personnel and weren't equipped to take on an entire city's worth of insurgents armed with RPGs and mortars. There were a lot of Monday-morning quarterbacks who thought they would have been braver, fought harder, and come home the heroes. Not one of them would ever have traded places with us in captivity.

We had brought shame to the Army and to the unit in many of their eyes. They wanted us to disappear, and far from enjoying all of the events and public appearances we were making, they wanted us to feel ashamed for having been POWs, for having been ambushed, and for having survived. The level of pettiness and bitterness I felt from other soldiers was staggering at times.

One place I always hated going was to the motor pool, the place where vehicle maintenance is performed, where all of our trucks are parked and maintained, where so many of the mechanics and technicians in the unit worked. Many of the people who had been killed in the ambush had worked in the motor pool. I needed to go there now and then, to fill out some paperwork or to take a driving test. Each time I went to the building that housed the maintenance bays, where mechanics wore grease-stained coveralls, I felt the absence of the men I knew who had worked there. In their place were other faces, people I barely knew, and I would be freshly reminded of the deaths of so many good people.

Today, you won't find the 507th Maintenance Company on a list anywhere on Fort Bliss. The unit no longer exists. It was deactivated and then reactivated under another name. It's now F Company of the Fifth Battalion, Fifty-second Air and Missile Defense (AMD). And even when there was talk of erecting a memorial to the brave soldiers who died that day, the discussions turned sour. The only memorial is a small bronze plaque on the side of the motor-pool building. A small plaque. It's as if they wish we would just disappear.

My whole time in captivity, I imagined myself staying in the Army, staying at Fort Bliss, raising my daughter, and making a life for myself. I imagined getting promoted to sergeant E-5 and progressing through the ranks, maybe getting more culinary arts training and making a career and a life in uniform. Even though I had never imagined myself doing anything else, after the resentment and pettiness became so blatant, I simply couldn't stay in the Army.

The pettiness didn't confine itself to the Army. Initially there had been reports that Jessica had fought bravely, had been fighting back and killing the enemy. And when those reports were proven false, there began to be speculation that I was angry and jealous of her for the way she was made to appear the hero. Some of the press speculated that she had become the Army's poster child because she was white and that I felt discriminated against.

I'm not sure how many times in interviews I have said that Jessica is my friend. I was her friend before that ambush and I'm still her friend now. I have never felt resentment toward her, not for the media hype about her role in the ambush and certainly not for any settlement she received for her injuries. I don't know why the Army or the press hyped up Jessica's role in the ambush. Judging from her testimony before Congress in 2007, it's clear that Jessica doesn't understand or appreciate the way the Army embellished her story.

And how could I be jealous of all of the unwanted attention she received? As difficult as it has been for me to handle the media attention, I'm sure Jessica had it much worse. There was speculation that I was jealous of her million-dollar book deal. I had very lucrative book and movie deals offered to me when I first got back, but I simply couldn't think in those terms, not for a long time. I think it's great that she could afford to go to school and work on beginning her career. She came from a very modest background and it's nice to know she was given a chance to make a good life for herself. After what she went through, how could I resent her for that?

Whatever the Army's reasons, I don't think their choice of Jessica for hero status had anything to do with color. Miller had only been in the Army about six months and everyone who survived can testify to the way he was returning fire. He was a brand-new private when he killed the enemy during his very first combat action in a disastrous convoy. Miller saved my life. If they were looking for an honest-to-goodness white hero, they had one in Private First Class Patrick Miller.

Miller received a Silver Star for his actions, but the Army refused to waive the required waiting period to promote him to specialist. In my opinion, the quiet Kansas man with the slow midwestern drawl is my redneck hero. He wasn't given near enough recognition for his actions that day. To come straight out of basic training and, in his very first battle, earn a Silver Star and not be acknowledged as the hero he is tells me that the hero business wasn't about someone being white.

I don't know why the Army chose to hype up Jessica's involvement in the ambush or why Miller is barely mentioned for his bravery. What I do know is that Lynch and Miller are both my friends and they are both deserving of any recognition they get.

My NCO from the DFAC, Sergeant Walters, was at first awarded a Bronze Star posthumously, but after a long investigation, it was upgraded to a Silver Star. There had been reports that a "blond" soldier had fought until his ammunition ran out. At first, the press thought the reports meant Jessica Lynch. But Sergeant Walters was blond and they say that he had been captured in a place where several empty magazines had been found. He was taken away and later executed. They say at the time of his capture, he had already been shot in the leg, shot twice in the back, stabbed twice in the abdomen, and had a dislocated left shoulder. Despite all of that, he continued to fight until he couldn't fight anymore.

He was finally awarded the Silver Star, but the Army failed to award him the V device that stood for valor in combat. Even Miller, who had killed so many of the enemy, didn't get the valor device. Eight people in the unit were given Bronze Stars, and only one of them had a V device. A big surprise to all of us was that the brigade commander, someone who wasn't even with us and as far as I know never saw combat while in Iraq, was awarded the Bronze Star with the V device at the end of his tour.

But who can know what goes through the minds of people who make such decisions? Lynch and Miller's experiences are just two examples of the poor judgment the Army has shown in the conduct of the war. Another example is what they did to the Pat Tillman story. The elaborate memorial ceremonies they held, the wildly overblown stories of Tillman's bravery, were an embarrassment. They wanted so badly to cover up that Pat Tillman had been killed by his own unit in Afghanistan. Not telling the truth about the incident was an insult to a family that had raised an outstanding, patriotic man. The family could have handled the truth of what happened. The lies the Army told are what put the family through hell.

Much of the resentment we felt from our fellow soldiers stemmed from the fact that some held us up as heroes. I don't know how many times I've tried to tell people that I'm not the hero. I was away from home only two months. There are soldiers in Iraq and Afghanistan who are spending fifteen months sweating and fighting and trying to survive away from their families. People have no idea how difficult it is to be gone so long. Then, when soldiers do finally get home, they spend even more time away from their families preparing and retraining to deploy a second or even third time. Over and over again they have gone. It's never-ending for them. They are the real heroes.

And there are so many people who were held prisoner in other wars, POWs who were in custody for years at a time, tortured and beaten, half starved and killed. Those are the real heroes.

The decision to write this book was a difficult one to reach. I finally agreed to do it after several people convinced me that it was important to tell my side of the story. So much has been said about me and my experience in the press and little of it has been very accurate. I always wonder who it is they are talking and writing about. It just couldn't be me.

My parents were the biggest supporters of the book idea and felt that it wasn't just that I should write a book, but that it was *important* for me to write it. They told me I needed to make sure my record in history was accurate and that folks heard my side of things. Of course they were convinced that my story would be a bestseller. A parent will always tell you you can do things whether it's within your capabilities or not. My parents were no different and had always told me that I could do anything I set my mind to, and while it's nice to get that kind of encouragement, I still knew those words were coming from my parents and they will always say what is best for their daughter. When that same advice started coming from someone like the Reverend Jackson, it was harder to write it off.

32

Reverend Jackson

Reverend Jesse Jackson contacted my family when I was in captivity to offer support. When I returned home, it was natural that he would call to offer his congratulations that I was safe and to wish me well. After that, he continued to be in touch, to call now and then to check in on me. He invited me to Chicago, where I met with people involved in his Rainbow/PUSH Coalition and he introduced me to several influential people.

It was at one of his events in Chicago that I met Michelle Obama. Of course no one knew at the time she would be first lady, but she and I were both on the agenda as speakers. I only met with her briefly, but later, I was in a group photo with her and several other prominent women. The photo became a big deal during the 2008 presidential campaign because Mother Khadijah Farrakhan, the wife of Nation of Islam leader Louis Farrakhan was also in the picture. Evidently, in some people's eyes, if you have your picture taken with someone, you must be in total agreement with them politically. I'm standing right next to Michelle in the photo with a big grin on my face.

Aside from introducing me to interesting people, Reverend Jackson was behind the scenes, mentoring me, offering advice from the moment I came home. He talked to me about my new role as a celebrity and explained the advantages and pitfalls of the new world I was living in. I was in the spotlight now, he explained, like it or not. I had to learn to live with the loss of privacy and the negative things that could come with it. He and his wife sort of took me under their wings and helped me with so many things. They, like no one else in my life, knew what it was to live this way and I was grateful for the time and effort they took to help.

"Listen to every word she says," my mother said after meeting Mrs. Jackson. "She knows what this life is like and you can learn a lot from her. So you listen to every word she says."

"Yes, Momma," I said. It was good advice and I have listened and learned a great deal from Mrs. Jackson. She has a firecracker of a personality and is very knowledgeable about the world and how to navigate within it. She is a great lady.

Reverend Jackson introduced me to his attorney, who offered me advice about some of those moneymaking opportunities that were coming my way. The last thing I wanted was to be taken advantage of and there were plenty of people out there who tried. Reverend Jackson and his attorney helped me wade through some of the offers, and while all the decisions were left to me to make, I felt confident that I had the information I needed to make good choices.

Then Reverend Jackson recommended me to his speakers' bureau. I was getting invitations to speak to a lot of different organizations. Some of them were charity events and I try to accept those at no charge when I can, but oftentimes large corporations and for-profit groups want to hear my story and the speakers' bureau helped me with those engagements. After I left the Army, it was a way of earning a living that felt acceptable to me. I learned to write a speech and to present my story and I worked at becoming good at it, so I figured I was performing and it was okay to get paid for that. And my family was telling me that people wanted to hear my story. I figured they were just my family saying the things that families say, but when Reverend Jackson told me I needed to go out in the public and tell my story, it was hard to ignore. I was reluctant to do it. I didn't think I was any different from any other soldier who had been through a difficult situation, but people seemed to want to hear how an ordinary person like me could get through such extraordinary events.

My mother, during a normal phone call with Reverend Jackson, mentioned that I was unhappy with the disability rating the Army board had assigned to me. I had already appealed the rating, but the appeal didn't result in any change. If there's one thing I know about Reverend Jackson, it's that if he can help, he will. He talked to me about the situation and my only fear was that it was going to turn into a big media issue if he became involved.

"Let's just not go too overboard with this," I cautioned.

When he did become involved, the press accused him of coming out of the woodwork to make a racial spectacle of the issue. They refused to see that he had been involved with me and my issues since before I had even returned home. He was simply a great friend doing what he could to help correct what he felt was an injustice.

The truth is, I didn't want the press involved at all in my dealings with the Army, but it was clear that my experience with the bureaucracy, like the experiences many veterans have had since returning home, had not been fair. The initial determination I received when I was medically retired from the Army was a 30 percent disability rating, the minimum amount for which you could be medically retired and still maintain benefits like post exchange and commissary shopping and the right to purchase Tricare insurance, the medical coverage military members and their families can use.

My biggest issue was that they refused to include any PTSD problems in their determination. It had already been abundantly clear that PTSD had been and was going to continue to be an obstacle for me. I was already on antidepressants and sleeping pills. I was seeing a therapist, I couldn't remember things, I was having nightmares—there was no doubt that I was suffering from PTSD and would be suffering from it for years to come. I was having these issues as a direct result of my service in uniform and there was no way the mental health portion of my medical issues should have been ignored. Despite all of that, the rating board determined that my PTSD issues should not factor into their calculations. The wording was something like: "Although your time in Iraq was trying, your mental condition is not ratable."

My time in Iraq was trying? I'll show you trying!

Reverend Jackson became involved in my case because he was a friend with connections who saw an injustice being committed. In fact, his high-profile involvement in my case was a very early indicator of the huge problems the Army was having with wounded soldiers. Hundreds of soldiers were having problems with their rating boards; different standards are used depending on where in the country your claim is filed, and even though veterans have suffered from PTSD after every war in history, the system is still having difficulty determining the long-term mental health effects individuals suffer. My issues with my disability rating were only a precursor to the growing scandal that would hit the Army later. The press wanted my issues to be about race and compared my experiences with Jessica's. In truth, the problems weren't just confined to me and went much, much deeper than race.

There was speculation that I was jealous of Jessica Lynch and her 70 percent disability rating. When Jessica and I talk, we ignore the ridiculous accusations and charges that have come out in the press. Besides, how could I be jealous of her? She suffered a broken back, a broken pelvis, and lay immobile in that Iraqi hospital for weeks. She is still suffering from her injuries. She's lucky she can even walk today. She deserves every penny she gets.

The only comparison that should be made between Jessica and me and our rating-board experiences is that her rating board automatically added points for PTSD. Her rating board said yes, her time in Iraq was also trying, so trying, in fact, that they automatically added points for what the experience *might* have done to her mentally. Jessica will tell you herself that she doesn't have nightmares, she isn't depressed, she's not suffering from the same kinds of mental health issues that I have. While my board said my issues were unratable, her rating board said hers were automatic. Automatic. *That,* I felt, was totally unfair.

After Reverend Jackson rattled some cages and after his attorney went with me for a visit before the board, my rating was changed to reflect the long-term effects of PTSD. It took more than two years for it all to be sorted out. Two years of paperwork and examinations and phone calls and meetings. The issue for me wasn't about the percentage rating or even about the money. The disability pay I get amounts to a fraction of Army specialist E-4 pay, and believe me, that's not a lot of money. The whole fight was about the Army recognizing that I was suffering from PTSD. I needed them to acknowledge that my mental health had suffered as a direct result of my service in the military. I wanted them to say out loud that the pills I was taking and the depression I was suffering and the therapy sessions I was attending were all a result of my service in Iraq. They had to say it. They finally did say it, and I'm grateful to Reverend Jackson for his help with the issue.

33

Recovery

For a long time, I had a recurring nightmare. One of the Iraqi guards would come to my house and knock on my door. I would picture him coming down the sidewalk and boldly knocking on the door as if it were perfectly normal, demanding that I let him in. I would wake up shivering and frightened. It always felt as if the guards were just about to invade my life again, to show up in my world, the world I tried to construct after them. The capture affected me in so insidious a way that most of the time I wasn't aware of the fears and anxieties it had caused.

When my belongings were stolen out of my truck during the ambush, one of the things I lost was a picture of my daughter. I hated the idea of her picture being in the hands of that mob. For the longest time I couldn't carry a picture of her with me for fear that someone would take it. I would rather not carry a photo of her than think of someone hostile having it. I carry her picture now, but that fear, that feeling that someone would take it away, was with me for a long time.

I had all kinds of little anxieties like that, feelings that were hard to talk about. I felt silly trying to describe why I couldn't carry a picture of my daughter, or why the doorbell ringing had so much fear associated with it. The fears were real and telling myself they were unnecessary didn't help.

Another thing I lost when my truck was ransacked was a disposable camera. I had taken pictures of our time in Camp Virginia, pictures of the convoy, pictures of my friends, some of whom are dead now. I wonder about that camera. Did someone find it and develop the pictures? The thought of a stranger having my pictures bothers me. Would they have just thrown the camera away? I would love to see those pictures now and I still wonder what happened to them.

For months after the capture, I would pop up in my sleep and, as it is described to me, I would flail my arms around as if I were fighting off attackers. My aunt Maggie saw it the most, in those first days when I was under her constant care, but for at least nine months, I had these episodes of fighting in the middle of the night. Sometimes I got out of bed and put my hands up in front of my face as if I were warding off blows. People said it looked like I was reliving those first moments after our capture when I was being kicked and beaten from all sides. Eventually the frequency of the episodes subsided, but I still have trouble sleeping and wonder, since I sleep alone most nights, whether the pop-up episodes continue now and then.

People may not ever ask me to my face, but I always know they wonder if I was raped. I get the impression that men I've dated recently have had the question in the back of their minds but don't ask it. I wasn't raped, but sometimes even I wonder about it. They say from her physical examinations that Jessica was sexually assaulted, but she doesn't remember it happening at all. Am I repressing some horrible memory, too? Could I have been raped that first day in those hours I was separated from the men? I had gone into shock and my memories are fuzzy during that period. There are large gaps in my memory that I've tried to fill in but can't. Do I remember everything that happened to me? My rational mind tells me that I wasn't raped, but sometimes a kind of psychosis takes over. There isn't any physical evidence to point to a sexual assault, but I wonder if some of my depression, some of my anxieties, are a result of an assault I'm working hard to forget. It's just something I wonder about.

After I got home, it was two years before I could even think about being with a man. I had been powerless in captivity and felt threatened all the time. It takes a willingness to be a little vulnerable to get involved with anyone, and I simply couldn't go there. When I did finally allow myself to be touched by a man, it was an old boyfriend, someone I was already familiar with. I couldn't trust anyone else.

I still have a hard time trusting men. Anyone who shows any interest, my first thought is to question their motives. What does he want from me? I feared that their only interest was my minor celebrity status and, at least once, that was exactly the case.

There are lots of things like that, things that had been easy before the capture but now suddenly aren't. I now have a difficult time remembering things. I have to set my cell-phone alarm to remind me to take medications and to remind me about appointments. There are alarms and bells all over my life now that have to be set or I'll forget that I have something on the stove or clothes in the wash, bills to pay, or even forget that I'm in the middle of a task that I'll wander away from.

Joe Hudson and Dave Williams tell me they have the same kinds of problems with remembering little things. I don't know where the problem comes from. I only know I'm not alone in this, so I figure it must have something to do with PTSD.

For the first year and a half or more after my release, I was almost manic about accepting invitations and attending events. The busier I was the less chance I had to stop and think about what had happened. For a long time, I had some kind of event or appearance to go to at least twice a month. Then, just after I got out of the military, with the recommendation of Reverend Jackson, I became registered with the speakers' bureau, which actively sought speaking appearances for me. The invitations to speak began to come in and that meant a lot of traveling. I was constantly on the go. I would have a very full schedule in February for Black History Month engagements and in March for Women's History Month events. Memorial Day, Veterans Day, and POW/MIA events were all times when my schedule was full of places to go and events to attend.

To be honest, through most of it, I felt like I was seeing everything through a fog. I don't know if it was all the medication I was taking or just residual effects from the capture, but I barely remember much of what I had been doing from day to day.

For almost the entire first year after my release, I needed almost constant help with medical care, getting around, and taking care of my daughter. I couldn't live on my own, so Janelle and I lived with my parents. I love my parents and appreciate everything they did for me, but after a year of living under their roof, it was easy to make the decision that it was time to leave. In 2004, about six months after I was medically discharged from the Army, I decided I should start shopping for a home of my own. My sister Nikki had recently bought a house and I decided it was time I did the same.

If it had been up to my father, I would still be in his house.

"You don't have any reason to leave," he said. "You can just stay right here."

As much as I appreciated his offer, I had to venture out on my own and find my own place for Janelle and me. I had considered moving to someplace in the Midwest, where there are open spaces and a chance to start over. I thought moving away from El Paso would be a good way to start fresh, to go someplace where I wasn't recognized and where I didn't have so much history. In the end, I decided staying near family, at least for a while, was the best idea.

I worked with a Realtor who showed me three houses and I bought the third one, just down the road from where my parents live. I used some of the fees I had earned through the speakers' bureau to buy furniture and to do some work in the kitchen, plant rose bushes in the backyard, and make other minor changes. Through all of it—the house search, the decision to buy, what it was like to actually sign all those papers to buy the house—I was in a complete daze. I barely remember it.

I was trying hard to put on a good face and appear as if everything was okay, but the foggy days lasted a long time. Keeping busy with the speaking engagements and other appearances helped me move through the fog. I could focus on something other than trying to figure out why I was feeling so dazed and out of sorts.

As the requests for engagements started to slow down and I had fewer things to keep me busy, depression set in and I had to start dealing with the day-to-day stuff I had so successfully avoided. A time finally came when I had an entire month without anything scheduled, an entire thirty-day period during which I didn't have to prepare a speech or show up at some event. I had been volunteering some time at Janelle's day-care center, but aside from that, I didn't have anything to do. I crashed big-time. I was in a deep depression and there were days when it was too much for me to even get out of the house. On those days, I would have to ask my parents to take Janelle to day care.

The phobias and fears, the depression and the guilt, all seemed to build on each other. Some days, it was hard to keep from crying over simply being alive. I was seeing a therapist every couple of weeks, but things weren't getting much better. These feelings of sadness have continued for years and I still struggle to understand why I am alive when so many good people aren't. Some days I'm okay, other days it's hard to simply walk out the door. I have felt as if I'm not really engaged in life. I'm not dating for the most part. I rarely go out. Sometimes it's hard to simply be around people.

Finally, in the spring of 2008, I checked myself into a psych ward for a few days. I had been crying for no reason, feeling depressed, and eventually I decided I needed help to bring myself out of the downward spiral.

Janelle knows that her mother has mood swings and I know that she watches me and worries. There is nothing I want more than to be a good mother to my little girl. I don't want her to see me in my down times, and I try to reassure her that everything will be okay. She'll hear me telling bits and pieces of stories about my life and she'll ask about it.

"That's when you were captured, right?" she will ask. I know that as she gets older, she'll have more questions and I hope I'll have the answers.

Large crowds bother me sometimes and I still battle with depression now and then. I can identify the worst of it earlier than before and I'm not afraid to call for help when I need it. I talk to my friend Theresa a lot and that helps. I keep in touch with the guys and we compare notes about the things we are feeling. I still think of Dave Williams as being kind of in charge, the go-to guy when I need help and advice. Miller sends me lots of text messages, sometimes dirty jokes that make me laugh when I need to the most. They usually have something to do with his redneck background and his countrified ways.

One day, I talked to him about something that had been eating at me. I often thought about missing that shot. I had fired at a man who had been trying to kill us but I missed. I told Miller that I worried that the man who got away from me may have killed people in my unit.

"You should be grateful that you missed," he said. "A day doesn't go by that I don't think about the people I killed. I remember every one of them."

Miller told me he killed eight of the men who ambushed our convoy. He had been riding with Riley and Private Brandon Sloan. Sloan had been hit in the head and died almost instantly. Shortly after their vehicle had been stopped, Miller had moved from position to position, killing as many as he could along the way. Three men had set up a mortar pit and were lobbing mortars into our convoy with devastating results. Miller shot all three of them.

"They made me watch them die," he said. After we had surrendered, his captors had dragged him back to the mortar pit. All three of the men had been mortally wounded but were still alive. Miller was made to watch them as they took their last breaths.

"I suppose if I hadn't killed them, they would have killed more of us, but it's hard," Miller said. "I don't know if it was a good thing or bad. You're lucky you didn't kill anybody."

"I would be dead if you hadn't done what you did," I told him. "It was them or us." But I know what I said didn't help much to ease the turmoil he goes through. Miller had joined the Army because of what happened on September 11, 2001. Did he understand then, when he signed on the dotted line, that there was a real possibility that he might actually have to kill someone?

The dirty jokes he sends to me in text messages are his way of telling me he's doing okay. He is still in the Army and seems to be doing fine.

I also keep up with what's going on with Hernandez. It's hard to believe that the young man I rode across the desert with is now a police officer. Hernandez is doing well in his new career and is starting a family with a wife and child. He has a book about the experience, too. It's called *American Hero: The Edgar Hernandez Story.* Personally, I think we should all write books. I think it's important to see the story from everyone's point of view. In any case, it usually helps me to talk with one of the guys when things are getting rough. They know what the deal is.

34

Life Today

I have an open invitation to attend the memorial service and ceremony Pie's family holds for her each year. They held the first service in 2004 but I wasn't able to attend. I had seen her bloody and battered in that truck. She had been alive at the time and there was nothing I could do to help her. It was hard for me to face the guilt of it. I knew in my heart that her family would not judge me, but I was afraid to look her children in the eye and be alive when their brave mother was dead.

In 2006 I finally decided I could attend the service. Lynch, Miller, and Hudson were all there. That year was the first time the sunrise service was held at the foot of a mountain formally known as Squaw Peak but that has since been renamed Piestewa Peak. For the event, the Piestewas invite family members of soldiers who were killed in Iraq or Afghanistan. Their names are read and all of them are memorialized along with Lori. I love how they use the ceremony as a way not only to honor Lori but also to help other families deal with their losses. And I think it's amazing that the mountain has been renamed to honor Lori. I can't think of a better way to memorialize that strong, brave woman who was as solid as a rock.

Sometimes I miss being in the Army. My life has taken a totally different direction than wearing the uniform and working my way through the military ranks, but I sometimes miss it. There's nothing that can replace the camaraderie of a military unit, that group of people you work with but who are also something of a family. I miss that companionship and closeness more than anything. I don't say that I regret leaving the Army, but I wish things had turned out differently.

Things are slowly, very slowly, going back to normal. There's no denying that my life is forever changed, not only because of what happened to me, but because of all of the media hype and attention that came after. I still do a lot of speaking engagements, and whenever there are POW or hostage issues in the news, my phone starts to ring again as news producers look for my take on the situation. As we approached the five-year anniversary of the war, my phone started ringing a lot and I'm sure each significant anniversary after that will be the same.

Some of the things I've been invited to do turned out to be opportunities to give back. Since I was invited to the *Glamour* Women of the Year event, I now get a vote for who is honored in future years. I get a packet in the mail that gives background information on each of the women that have been nominated for the award. It's fascinating to read about so many strong women who have done great things. I have gone to the event in New York each year and love meeting everyone and being part of the event.

I was invited to speak at a Veterans Administration–sponsored health conference in Las Vegas to tell them about my experiences with the system. I spoke to them frankly about my problems with my ratings, the problems I faced getting a fair rating of my PTSD, and how my experiences might be used as an example of what changes could be made to improve the process.

After I spoke at the conference, the director of minority affairs for the VA asked me to serve on its advisory board. I hesitated at first, not sure what I could contribute to such a board, but she assured me my personal experience and the input of someone from the current conflict would be helpful. So now, once a year, I travel with board members to different parts of the country, where we look at VA systems and offer recommendations for improving services for minorities. We go to briefings in Washington, D.C., each fall and then make site visits in the spring and work together to try to find solutions to problems.

It feels good to know that some of the issues I've raised with the board will be acted on, and even after only a short time I know that my perspective has been helpful. I was surprised to learn that I would be the first person on the board who represents the current conflict since so many of the issues of today are completely different than they had been for other wars. All of the other committee members are from the Vietnam, Korean, and First Gulf War conflicts, so I provide a younger, more current perspective.

For example, I reminded the board that this conflict represents the first in which large numbers of female veterans will have actually gone through combat and suffered combat injuries. The equipment they use for women's physical therapy isn't always the same as the equipment for men. Not to mention that many of the female veterans will want to have babies. I wondered how many VA hospitals are prepared to handle deliveries or were even equipped with maternity wards. The answer was, not many. I hope my questions helped get the board thinking about the subject.

One of the first trips I made with the board was to a VA clinic that was located near a reservation where a majority of the patients were African-American and Native American. Despite the pre-ponderance of Native American patients, only a small percentage of the staff of the clinic was Native American. We had long dis-cussions about whether that imbalance in clinic staff would affect patient care and whether some issues felt by the Native American community might be missed because of a lack of understanding and personal perspective.

That's just one example of the issues we address when we are sent out on our site visits. Of course, I'm interested in how the clinics are equipped to care for so many veterans who are facing years of treatment for PTSD and how those issues are rated and treated in the VA system. I hope my experiences with the system can help take some of the pain out of the bureaucratic process.

I still speak to all of the guys regularly. When I need the voice of wisdom, I still call Dave to talk over things. Ron checks in often and we exchange e-mails and phone calls. I'll check in on Hernan-dez and his new wife and child. Patrick calls all the time, some-times sends me text messages, and still doesn't hesitate to send me dirty jokes. One recently went like this:

"Here's a redneck pickup line: Baby, do you own a chicken farm? Because you sure know how to raise a cock."

Sometimes I don't know what to do with that Patrick.

I don't get invited to attend the events that take place on Fort Bliss anymore. Not for Veterans Day, not for Memorial Day, not even when they have POW/MIA day; the Army post that is just down the road from me doesn't invite me to attend. Just before the event, I can usually expect a call from Joe Hudson.

"Are you gonna go?" Hudson will ask.

"Yeah, I'll go if you go," I'll say, and we'll both just show up and attend the ceremony that is meant to honor people who have been taken prisoner or are still missing in action. It's kind of ironic really. We're two local POWs of the most recent conflict and we don't even get invited.

On the personal side, I went back to school and earned my associate's degree. I'm taking culinary arts classes now and my dream is to be a kick-ass baker. I want to make specialty cakes, beautiful pieces of art that folks can eat. I would love to cater special events and make one-of-a-kind cakes that will be part of the memories of someone's special occasion. I'm pretty good at it, but I want to get better. Every once in a while, I'll take a cake to Janelle's school or make something for special family occasions. I plan to study hard and really work at perfecting my craft.

I've found that cooking and entertaining for a small crowd is a big mood changer for me. Having a few friends over for dinner, fixing something special, and making them happy with my food and drink helps clear away the cobwebs and gets me in a better mood. This year, I threw a little party for Theresa's birthday, complete with grilled steaks and watermelon martinis. It was nice to do something special for my girlfriend and making something delicious and talking with friends is sometimes just what the doctor ordered.

Janelle is growing up to be a very smart and independent young lady. I'm so proud of her. She asks me questions about my experiences sometimes, but I think she treads lightly, for fear a question might bring on one of my sad moods. I hope this book will give her and everyone who reads it a complete picture of what we ex-POWs went through and how the experience has affected my life.

I love being a mother and would really like to expand my family, find a man to share my life with, and have another child. There are so many times when I've mentally given up on that dream. I figured I'll never find the right guy, never make that connection with anyone that will last the rest of my life. Feelings for the old boyfriend who is now married and has two kids creep back when I consider the impossibility of finding that special person. My friends tell me not to give up and I try not to, but it's hard. It's just really hard.

The guys and I all schedule our annual POW exams at the same time in Florida so we can get together and make a reunion of it. The exams are part of a Defense Department POW study. We aren't required to be involved but none of us have opted out. John McCain is part of the same study, as are lots of other Vietnam-era veterans. So once a year we all get together and go through the extensive tests and get caught up on each other's lives.

We went through twenty-two days of hell together in 2003, days none of us will forget, days that make us connected one way or another. Hardly a day goes by when I don't think about the Iraqi civilians who are caught up in this conflict who want a better life for their children. I think about the men who were kind to us, like the guard who slept outside my door, and especially the three police officers who were with us in the end, Raymond and the Captain and the Major. I hope that they didn't suffer any consequences for helping us. I wonder if they were the ones who told the Marines where to find us.

One of the Marines involved with my rescue made a connection with me on my Facebook page recently.

"I don't know if you remember me," he wrote.

At first I didn't recognize his picture, his civilian clothes, his beard, and his longer, un-Marine-like hair. But then I could see the young Randy Meyers, who had been one of the brave guys who helped to free us. I was happy to hear from him and enjoy the connections the social-networking page allows.

Martin the Marine, the one I dreamed of so often, is another

Facebook friend. I haven't told him about all the dreams I had of him when I was in captivity. That might be too embarrassing. It's just nice to have him back as a friend even if it is just as a cyber-friend.

The 2008 election presented me with some hard choices. I had always admired John McCain. No one could deny his bravery as a POW, and since he had been born in Panama, in my family he was always considered a fellow Panamanian. At first, it was natural for me to throw my support behind him. Someone from McCain's campaign did call me and ask if I would appear at one of his election events. I had to turn it down because I've never wanted to get involved in politics. They were very kind and understanding about my desire not to get involved in that way.

I've never been very political but the last election had so much at stake. Over time, I came to believe that Senator McCain's time had passed and it was time for the country to go in a new direction. Barack Obama convinced me he was the right man for the job. Like most of the country, I have great hopes for his administration.

Iraq was a major issue in the campaign and I think most people supported Obama because of his promise to get us out of there as soon as possible. The pundits worry that if we leave too soon, the Iraqis will suffer even more violence and innocent people will be killed. I figure the Iraqis lived through thirty years of a brutal dictatorship. Saddam Hussein put that country and its people through hell. If they could survive under that regime, they can survive just about anything. People like Raymond and the Captain and the kind old man have convinced me that the Iraqis want a good life, and yes, they have humanity. I think about the Iraqis who helped us and hope that they can one day live in a peaceful country.

And of course, hardly a day goes by when I don't think about the ones in my unit who didn't make it. There's not much I can do but remember them. We should all remember them.

SPECIALIST JAMAAL ADDISON, 22
SERGEANT EDWARD ANGUIANO, 24
SERGEANT GEORGE BUGGS, 31
FIRST SERGEANT ROBERT DOWDY, 38
PRIVATE RUBEN ESTRELLA-SOTO, 18
PRIVATE FIRST CLASS HOWARD JOHNSON III, 21
SPECIALIST JAMES KIEHL, 22
CHIEF WARRANT OFFICER JOHNNY VILLAREAL MATA, 35
PRIVATE FIRST CLASS LORI PIESTEWA, 23
PRIVATE BRANDON SLOAN, 19
SERGEANT DONALD WALTERS, 33

The Army's official report of the attack on the 507th Maintenance Company can be found at this website: www.army.mil/features/507thMaintCmpy/.